Enabling Environments in the Early Years

Making provision for high quality and challenging learning experiences in early years settings

by Liz Hodgman

Contents

Published by Practical Pre-School Books, A Division of MA Education Ltd,
St Jude's Church, Dulwich Road, Herne Hill, London, SE24 0PB.

Tel: 020 7738 5454

www.practicalpreschoolbooks.com

© MA Education Ltd 2011

All photos © MA Education Ltd. Photos taken by Ben Suri.

Front cover (clockwise): © iStockphoto.com/Dmitry Naumov, © iStockphoto.com/Quavondo,
© MA Education Ltd 2011

All rights reserved. No part of this publication may be reproduced, stored in a retrieval system, or transmitted by any means, electronic, mechanical, photocopied or otherwise, without the prior permission of the publisher.

ISBN 978-1-907241-18-5

Early Childhood Essentials

Why is the environment important in supporting children's learning?

This book is for all early years practitioners and aims to support managers and staff to develop the learning environment for the children in their setting. It will be useful for practitioners in nurseries, pre-schools, children's centres, home-based settings and schools.

What is an enabling environment in the early years?

It is a physical indoor and outdoor environment which provides:

- Space
- High quality resources
- Displays
- Accessibility
- Stability

All of which are designed to promote young children's physical, mental and emotional health and wellbeing.

It is also an emotional environment providing warmth and acknowledgement of each child as unique. A truly enabling environment ought to support children's learning across the six areas of learning of the Early Years Foundation Stage, and ensure that each child is "a competent learner from birth who can be resilient, capable, confident and self-assured" (EYFS (2007), *Practice Guidance for the Early Years Foundation Stage*. DCSF, page 5).

Why is the environment so important?

The environment plays a key role in supporting and developing a child's learning and development. An enabling environment will:

- Provide a child with stimulation and challenge.

- Pick up on a child's interests and enable them to explore and experiment.

- Be flexible to allow for quiet, reflective and focused learning, maybe in a comfortable book corner, as well as more boisterous and physical play.

- Support children's learning across all six aspects of learning, allowing them to practise their skills and develop new ones.

- Help children to learn about rules and how to communicate with others.

- Encourage children's creativity and imagination and permit them to take risks and make mistakes.

- Promote equality and support children to develop a greater understanding of others' needs, cultures, religions and backgrounds.

- Provide safety and emotional support.

- Encourage independence and help children to develop a positive attitude towards learning.

Every child matters

Providing an enabling environment links to the five Every Child Matters outcomes:

- **Stay Safe:** an enabling environment provides children with a safe and secure place to play and learn, with support from caring adults who will continually risk assess and evaluate the environment, help children to learn about dangers, and how to protect themselves.

- **Be Healthy:** an enabling environment provides children with support to develop good personal hygiene practices, such as hand washing, and a clean place to play, reducing the spread of infections.

- **Enjoy and Achieve:** an enabling environment provides a range of activities and resources that are stimulating and encourage participation, support learning and development, challenge, and the opportunity to succeed.

- **Make a Positive Contribution:** an enabling environment encourages children and parents to make contributions, where their voices are listened to and acted upon, where they are consulted about changes and developments in their setting.

- **Achieve Economic Well Being:** an enabling environment that offers challenge; where children learn and develop, gaining skills to support them in later learning and eventually in employment and adult life, enabling them to achieve economic wellbeing.

To access The Every Child Matters Outcomes Framework (DCSF, 2008) visit http://www.dcsf.gov.uk/childrensplan/downloads/ECM%20outcomes%20framework.pdf

The environment: different approaches and curricula

The environment has always been considered important in children's learning and development, and features in the research and approaches of the main theorists. It is also a principle of many early education curricula and frameworks across the world. The below lists summarise the importance that key theorists, followed by early years frameworks in the UK, place on the early learning environment.

Maria Montessori (1870-1952) was an Italian physician and educator who developed the Montessori method of educating children based on her research and experiences educating children from the slums of Rome. A key aspect of the Montessori approach is based on providing children with the freedom to learn in an environment prepared with materials and resources designed to enable children to direct their own learning. The environment is uncluttered and all resources are clearly labelled and at child-height so that each child can pick their own resources. The Montessori approach firmly believes in free flow between the indoors and outdoors, with the outdoor space being prepared for the children to encourage exploration and independent activity.

Jean Piaget (1896-1980), child psychologist, held a theory that when children interacted with their physical and social environments, they were organising the information gained into groups and interrelated ideas, 'schemes'. He thought that when children met something new in their environment they had to either put that learning into an existing scheme or make a new one for it. For example during what Piaget termed the Sensorimotor phase (which lasts from birth to two years of age) children learn about their environment using their senses and motor skills. They learn about their parents or caregivers or a favourite toy. Then children learn that these people or toys still exist even though they are unable to touch them or see them, through games such as peek-a-boo. This theory of schemas had a significant impact on how teachers and early educators viewed the importance of the environment on children's learning.

Lev Vygotsky (1896-1934) was a Russian psychologist, who later became incredibly influential in educational theory. In 1935 Vygotsky delivered a lecture on 'The problem of the environment' during which he contended that the human brain, unlike an animal's brain which merely reacts to the environment, has the capacity to alter the environment for their own purposes. He believed that the social and cultural environments in which the children were raised in played a key role in the child's learning.

Rudolf Steiner (1861-1925) was an Austrian philosopher who developed a different style of educating children. The Steiner approach is very much based on providing a suitable environment, with lots of natural and sensory resources. In Steiner settings there are no hard corners, plastic or brightly coloured toys and resources. Wherever possible Steiner settings use natural resources such as wood, sheep's fleeces and beeswax crayons. The resources are usually chosen to be able to be used in a variety of ways and so encourage exploration and creativity, for example open-ended resources such as wooden blocks or logs, pieces of plain cloth, feathers etc. The Steiner approach is also very much focussed on practical and domestic activities. The day is very structured, and whilst outdoor play is promoted, it is not free flow play but at an allocated slot on the timetable.

Following World War II, the educational philosophy now known as **The Reggio Emilia Approach** was developed in Italy. Its approach to teaching young children puts the natural development of children, as well as the close relationships that they share with their environment, at the centre of its philosophy. In fact the emphasis on the environment in this approach is so great that the learning environment is often described as the 'third teacher'. A typical Reggio Emilia environment will include mirrors, photographs, plants and lots of light. Specially designed pre-schools have classrooms that open onto a central piazza area, with wall sized windows and doors onto courtyards and outdoor classrooms. The environment is designed to inform and engage the user, with displays and photographs of the children's work with captions of discussions between adults and children. There is a real community feel to the environment with shared spaces and resources.

In more recent years **Urie Bronfenbrenner** constructed the Ecological Systems Theory, which is based on how different environments impact on people's lives. Bronfenbrenner describes the 'Micro System', or a child's home or setting, as where the most amount of learning takes place. The child is not a passive recipient of experiences but actively involved and helping to construct the environment.

In 1996 New Zealand developed their **Te Whaariki** curriculum. One of the key elements of this framework was the scope for childhood education providers to develop their own programme within the Te Whaariki curriculum, to meet the needs of the local traditions and environments.

The Early Years Foundation Stage

The Early Years Foundation Stage, (DCSF, 2007) the framework for children aged 0-5 in England, also values the environment, evidenced by its four principles:

A Unique Child: every child is a competent learner from birth who can be resilient, capable, confident and self-assured.

Positive Relationships: children learn to be strong and independent from a base of loving and secure relationships with parents/and or a key person.

Enabling Environments: the environment plays a key role in supporting and extending children's development and learning.

Learning and Development: children develop and learn in different ways and at different rates and all areas of learning and development are equally important and inter-connected.

Principles into Practice Cards: Enabling Environments

The EYFS framework principles are further broken down into statements on the Principles into Practice Cards, which form part of the EYFS pack. They reflect the importance of the environment to support children's learning and development. These four key areas cover the importance of using the observation, assessment and planning cycle to provide an environment that meets the needs and interests of each child; that provides challenge and stimulation to support their learning and development and engages with the wider community to support their holistic development towards the five Every Child Matters Outcomes.

The Cards state:

- *3.1 Observation, Assessment and Planning: Babies and young children are individuals first, each with a unique profile of abilities. Schedules and routines should flow with the child's needs. All planning starts with observing children in order to understand and consider their current interests, development and learning.*

- *3.2 Supporting Every Child: The environment supports every child's learning through planned experiences and activities that are challenging but achievable.*

- *3.3 The Learning Environment: A rich and varied environment supports children's learning and development. It gives them the confidence to explore and learn in a secure and safe, yet challenging, indoor and outdoor space.*

- *3.4 The Wider Context: Working in partnership with other settings, other professionals and with individuals and groups in the community supports children's development and progress towards the outcomes of Every Child Matters;*

being healthy, staying safe; enjoying and achieving; making a positive contribution and economic well-being.

How the other principles of the EYFS link to the Enabling Environment

A Unique Child

This principle focuses on providing an environment that supports each child to develop a sense of their own identity and culture and of those around them. It should support each child's emotional needs, recognising and praising both effort and achievement as well as promoting a sense of belonging. The staff need to enable children to learn by doing for themselves rather than showing or telling them. Activities need to follow their interests and needs (including physical needs).

There needs to be an ethos of listening to children and valuing their contributions. Families need to feel welcome and supported when accessing the setting. Children need to feel safe but be given support to assess dangers and take reasonable risks. Children should be given the opportunity to make choices within a framework of boundaries, rules and limits that the children are supported to understand.

Positive Relationships

This principle focuses on providing an environment that is inclusive and respecting of everyone's differences. Staff ought to listen to and support the development of professional relationships with parents, as well as involving them in their child's progress and development. Additional support should be offered for those with low literacy skills or EAL. For children this will include active listening, including very young babies and providing emotional safety so they are able to respond positively to challenges without fear of failure or ridicule, building on prior learning. A key worker will help to develop secure attachments, promote independence and support a child's transitions within and beyond the setting.

Learning and Development

This principle focuses on providing an environment that encourages physical and emotional play, alone or with others, that is challenging, interesting, attractive and accessible with child-initiated and adult-led activities.

It needs to offer space and time for the children to explore resources that are flexible. It should allow children to make decisions. Staff need to have realistic expectations of each child and encourage connections, especially between experiences at home, the setting and the wider community. It should promote sustained shared thinking between adults and children. It also needs to promote tidying up and putting away of resources by the children.

KEY POINTS IN WHY THE ENVIRONMENT IS IMPORTANT IN SUPPORTING CHILDREN'S LEANING

- An Enabling Environment will provide space, high quality resources, displays, accessibility and stability for the children

- The environment supports children's learning and development:
    - across all six areas of learning
    - across the five Every Child Matters Outcomes

- The Enabling Environment includes the indoor and outdoor spaces and the emotional environment

- The environment is one of the four key principles of the Early Years Foundation Stage; Enabling Environments

Chapter 1

Auditing your setting's current provision

Ofsted's Leading to Excellence Article describes stimulating environments as:

> Adults plan the day carefully, tailoring the arrangements to meet each child's welfare and learning needs. They plan the use of space available inside and out to maximise its impact on outcomes for children. The timing of activities and how children move around is well coordinated. Appropriate resources are available and easily accessible to promote children's all-round development. Risks are assessed and managed well, enabling children to freely choose activities, test their skills and make new discoveries within safe boundaries.
> Ofsted, (2008) *Early Years Leading to Excellence*

Whatever type of setting you work in there will be times when you want to make changes to the environment. This might be because you have been given funding or a grant to make improvements, a change in the space you are allocated, you want to introduce a new activity or resource, or you just feel like a change or a turn around.

The starting point for making any changes to current provision is to look at what is already in place. Auditing the provision will enable managers and practitioners to use a systematic approach to establishing what is already available in their environment and what areas need to be further developed, strengthened and enhanced. It should also provide some valuable information for the settings Self Evaluation Form and evidence for a future Ofsted Inspection.

The environment and the Self Evaluation Form

The Ofsted Self Evaluation Form (SEF) is available to complete online at www.ofsted.gov.uk or you can download a copy. (Reference 080104, published September 2009) A guidance document is also available to download to support practitioners in its completion. (Reference 080103, published September 2009)

It is important to remember that completing a Self Evaluation Form is not simply a question of ticking boxes, rather it is a question of reflecting on the services offered, assessing their delivery, and then evaluating what impact they have had on the children's learning and development. The table on page 9 outlines the key areas of the Ofsted SEF that link directly to the environment, and details of where supporting information can be found for each requirement within this book.

See page 9 for the environment and the Self Evaluation Form.

Audit of current provision

The following pages provide guidance on auditing various areas of your provision, to provide you with either an individual assessment of one aspect, or completed as a set to produce a holistic picture of the setting. A sample checklist on the general learning environment has been fully laid on page 10, with room for comments on whether each aspect of the learning environment has either been fully developed, partially developed or needs developing. For other aspects of provision such as the outdoor environment, we have provided a list of areas for you to assess and to form your own checklists.

These checklists can be completed by the manager or a senior practitioner/room leader or as a staff team. Using time during a staff meeting to look at one of the checklists will bring fresh ideas and viewpoints. It is very easy to miss things when you are in a familiar environment every day. For example, the nursery nurse in the baby room of a large day nursery will be able to give a different perspective on how she sees the outdoor area for the toddler room. The Practice Guidance for the EYFS promotes involving all staff working together as a team to

An environment that stimulates the children's senses

Free flow, the children choose where they want to be

'sustain a successful learning environment' (DCSF, 2007, page 12). Childminders working alone might consider asking a fellow childminder to complete the form with them, or maybe one of their minded parents or their Network Co-ordinator.

An audit will provide you with information on:

- What you are doing well

- Areas that need to be improved upon or developed

- Areas that you may not previously considered

It is important to remember that completing these checklists provides a snapshot of the provision at that moment in time. As such they will need to be revisited annually. This will provide a good record of the development of the setting and the continued progress that it is making in improving its environment.

Wherever possible include notes of evidence to support your responses as this will be useful when planning future developments and improvements. For example on the general checklist, 'Is the environment safe and secure?' include how you have secured boundaries, doors etc. List safety measures you have put in place and refer to risk assessments.

General learning environment checklist

The general learning environment checklist provides an overview of the key areas and is a good starting point before embarking on the more focused checklists that follow.

The first list will help you consider areas such as accessibility. This includes how accessible the setting is for children and/ or parents with Special Educational Needs or other needs, for example English as a second language. It will help your setting to focus on removing or helping overcome barriers to enable all children to develop and fulfil their potential. This is explored in greater detail in the Equality of Opportunity Checklist on page 12.

Providing challenge is another area on the checklist. When completing this you will need to consider how you provide challenge to children across the different age ranges and abilities, including those with Special Educational Needs (SEN) and the gifted and talented. Challenges should also consider across the six areas of learning (EYFS). Challenges can be thought of as the next steps to help the child move onto the next stage of their learning and development. Challenges need to be achievable but stretching.

Balancing adult led and child-initiated activities is very important and the checklist encourages discussion around children being able to choose their own activities and flexibility in planning to allow changes to follow a child's lead. Chapter Two, The Indoor Environment, provides information and case studies around children choosing their own activities. See page 10 for the general learning environmental checklist.

Indoor environment checklist

The Indoor Environment Checklist encourages a more focused evaluation on the indoor environment including storage, use of space, safety and displays. Chapter Two, The Indoor Environment, provides more detailed information and case studies, including how different settings have tackled storage issues and how these can be effectively used to support children's tidying up and literacy development. The below list indicates aspects of the indoor environment that need assessing in your audit:

- Does the indoor environment support all six areas of learning?
  - Communication, language and literacy development
  - Personal, social and emotional development
  - Physical development
  - Knowledge and understanding of the world
  - Problem solving, reasoning and numeracy
  - Creative development

- Does the environment support child-initiated activities?

- How do you balance providing a 'homely' environment alongside space to be boisterous and do large physical activities?

- How do you store resources so that they are easily accessible?

- How can children chose their own resources and activities?

- How do you involve children in tidying away?

- How is wall space utilised for displays and information sharing?

- How do you display children's artwork?

- How is the space shared for the differing needs of babies, toddlers or pre-school children?

- How often do you change the indoor provision? For example the role play area?

- How do you provide a quiet place for children to relax and chat?

- How do you risk assess the indoor environment?

- How do you teach the children about safety indoors?

- How is the indoor space planned to allow children to play, rest/sleep and eat?

Outdoor environment checklist

The Outdoor Environment Checklist includes discussion points on how the weather can impact on provision, taking risks and sustainability. Chapter Three, The Outdoor Environment, includes a case study on a Children's Centre's eco-garden and how it was extended to include a farm shop role play area to further enhance the learning of the children. The below list indicates aspects of the outdoor environment that need assessing in your audit:

- Does the outdoor environment support all six areas of learning?
  - Communication, language and literacy development
  - Personal, social and emotional development
  - Physical development
  - Knowledge and understanding of the world
  - Problem solving, reasoning and numeracy
  - Creativity

- Does the environment support child-initiated activities?

- Do you make good use of natural resources in the outdoor environment? Think about:
  - Weather/the elements
  - Ground

- Do you provide role-play resources outdoors?

- Do you maximise the use of boundary fencing and walls?

- Do you provide outdoor experiences for babies?

- How environmentally friendly is your outdoor space? Consider use of water butts, compost bins etc.

- How do you support children to access the outdoors if they are not appropriately attired?

The environment and the Self Evaluation Form

Area of the Self Evaluation Form	Detail requested by the Self Evaluation Form	Evidence that could be included	Advice to be found in this book
Part A: **Setting details and views of those who use the setting** **Section 1:** **Your setting**	Ofsted recommend that every setting includes information on the building, the rooms and areas and how they are used. Addressing in particular the accessibility of outdoor space, general accessibility within the setting, stairs, ramps etc and any other relevant information about the structure of the environment.	Brief detail of each room, ages of the children it is used for and activities provided. Is the setting on one level? If not how is the upstairs made accessible to the children of different ages and abilities?	See Chapter One, Auditing your setting's current provision. See page 28 for information on freeflow and making the outdoor space more accessible.
Part B: **The quality and standards of the early years provision** **Section 3:** **Quality of the provision**	• Plan the learning environment to help children progress towards the early learning goals. • Plan children's play and exploration, in and out of doors, with a balance of adult-led and child-led activities that helps children to think critically and be active and creative learners. • Plan for individual children, taking into account their culture and background, including the needs of any children with SEN and/or disabilities and those learning EAL. • Offer an inclusive and welcoming service to all children. • Ensure the suitability and safety of outdoor and indoor spaces, furniture, equipment and toys.	Refer to your planning documents and give examples of where you have made changes in the environment to support a particular child or group of children to progress towards the early learning goals taking into account their particular needs. Examples of how the environment has been developed to support different ethnicities, cultures, language and abilities. Multicultural toys and resources, posters reflecting the diversity of the setting, books and writing in different languages, accessibility etc. Results of parental survey on how welcoming the setting is. Risk assessments. Details of staff training around health and safety.	See pages 22-26 and 36-39 at the end of the Indoor and Outdoor Environment Chapters for specific ideas for each area of learning. See Auditing your setting's current provision chapter. See the diversity and equality of opportunity checklists on page 12. Emotional environment chapter (see page 45 for information on creating a welcoming environment). Risk assessments see page 61.
Section 4: **Outcomes for children**	This section is linked to the five Every Child Matters (ECM) outcomes: • Achieve and enjoy • Feel safe • Adopt healthy lifestyles • Make a positive contribution • Develop skills for the future	Information on displays that support the 5 ECM outcomes. Visual routines. Risk Assessments and safety notice. Information on how the environment has been developed to support children to make their own choices and decisions and to develop independence.	See the ECM outcomes on page 3 of this book for more information on how each outcome links to enabling environments.
Section 5: **The leadership and management of the early years provision**	• The quality of the environment and how effectively the provider uses space within the provision.	This section could include how you as a leader have evaluated the environment and what steps you have taken to improve it.	The advice on writing checklists on pages 6-14 could be used as supporting evidence for this during the inspection

Section 5: The leadership and management of the early years provision	• The extent to which adults ensure the learning environment and resources are available to all children. • How inclusive and welcoming is your service? • How accessible is your building? • The quality and effectiveness of risk assessments and actions you take to manage or eliminate risks. • How are the premises kept safe and secure so that children cannot leave alone or others gain unsupervised access?	Discuss how you deploy resources and how well you promote equality, accessibility and diversity. Audit of Equality of Opportunity (see page 12). Detail access arrangements. Staff training on managing risks. Examples of how risks have been effectively managed. Signing in procedures for staff and visitors to the setting.	Chapter 5 provides detail on how to evaluate and make changes to the environment. See page 17 on how storage can enable children to choose their own activities and resources. See page 45 in the Emotional Environment Chapter. See page 61 for risk assessments See page 35 for examples of how settings have managed risks effectively.
Section 6: The overall effectiveness of the early years provision	This section provides an opportunity for you to explain how you have improved the environment and how this has supported the setting to meet the children's individual needs.	Brief outline of process of evaluating the environment, identifying areas for improvement, consultation with children and parents and resulting changes.	The chapter on Developing the Environment includes ideas for making changes to the environment.

General learning environment checklist

Aspect	Needs developing	Partly developed	Fully developed
Is the environment welcoming?			
Is the environment safe and secure?			
Does it provide positive images of gender, ethnicity, language, religion, culture and abilities?			
Is it accessible?			
Does the environment offer the children challenge?			
Does the environment stimulate the children's senses? (Touch, smell, hearing, sight and taste)			
Are the children able to choose their own activities?			
Are the children able to be involved in tidying away?			
Are the children able to move freely between the indoor and outdoor environment?			
Is the environment flexible so that a child's lead can be followed?			
Does the environment support the children's: • Communication, language and literacy development • Personal, social and emotional development • Physical development • Knowledge and understanding of the world • Problem solving, reasoning and numeracy • Creativity			
Does the environment support children to develop independence skills?			
Is the environment regularly reviewed?			

- Are children encouraged and supported to take risks?

- How is the outdoor environment risk assessed?

- How do you overcome staff/parents resistance to outdoor play when the weather in inclement?

- How do you store outdoor resources?

- Have you provided space for children to relax and chat outdoors?

Emotional environment checklist

The emotional environment checklist focuses on how the environment, both physical as well as your setting's staff, support children's personal, social and emotional development. One area on the checklist is 'Can all children make choices?' Being able to make decisions is an important part of everyday adult life. Children can be supported to develop independent thinking from an early age, providing that staff offer choices. Choice is not just about providing children with different toys and resources to play with, but should be woven into all aspects of children's care and education. You should give children the opportunity to be able to choose what activity to engage in, as well as when and how, and to what level of engagement. Chapter four discusses why the emotional environment is vital to a child's all round development and provides ideas and activities to support it. These include visual routines and visual systems for celebrating effort and achievement (see page 49). The Every Child Matters framework stresses the importance of parents understanding and supporting their child's emotional needs and Chapter four provides suggested activities to help settings share ideas and resources with parents. The below list indicates aspects of the emotional environment that need assessing in your audit:

- How are children and parents welcomed to the setting?

- Do the resources available reflect the diversity of the children and adults within the setting and in the local community?

- Are there welcome posters in different languages?

- Can all children make choices?

- Can children leave an activity and return to it later?

- Do the resources available support children's emotional development?

- Are photographs of the children displayed?

- Are the children's names displayed?

- Are pieces of the children's named artwork displayed?

- Is there somewhere special that each child can keep its own belongings? (A bag on a peg for example)

- Are photographs of staff displayed for the children to see?

- Are there places within the setting where children can sit and talk?

- Are the children provided with visual routines? (See page 49 for examples of visual routines)

- Are the setting's 'rules' displayed visually to the children?

- Is there a visual system for celebrating effort and achievements?

- How are staff supported who are emotionally exhausted from working with children with deep sadness, anger or frustration?

Free flow checklist

Providing free flow between the indoor and outdoor environment can present many challenges to staff. The checklist provides some points to consider and the concept is explored in greater depth in chapter three, The Outdoor Environment. The below list indicates aspects of the free flow provision that need assessing in your audit:

- Is the outside area always accessible to the children?

- Are doors always open so children can come and go as they please between the outdoors and inside?

- Is there suitable protection from the weather available to children and staff? Welly boots? Waterproof clothing? Coats? Umbrellas?

- Is the outdoor area staffed at all times?

Suitably dressed for the weather

A welcome poster in different languages

- Do adults in the setting view inclement weather as a hindrance? Or an exciting opportunity?

- Are all of the six areas of learning of the EYFS covered both inside and outside each day?

Restricted or no outdoor space checklist

Restricted or no outdoor space is a checklist for settings that have limited or no outdoor space accessible to them at their own premises. The Practice Guidance to the EYFS, (2007) page 7, states 'If a setting does not have direct access to an outdoor play area then they must make arrangements for daily opportunities for outdoor play in an appropriate nearby location.' Some of the issues this raises are addressed in chapter three, The Outdoor Environment, including a risk assessment for daily outings and some suggestions for alternative outdoor play spaces. The list below indicates aspects of restricted or no outdoor space that need assessing in your audit.

- How do you ensure children have access to the outdoor environment every day?

- How is it incorporated into the planning?

- How is the children's safety managed in public outdoor spaces?
  - Risk Assessments
  - Policies and procedures
  - Equipment

Equality of opportunity checklist

The equality of opportunity checklist looks at how accessible the setting is, both physically and linguistically, for those for whom English is not their first language, or with low-level literacy skills. It links with the Equality Act 2010 which came into effect on 1st October 2010 and replaces the large part of the Disability Discrimination Act (DDA) 1995. The Equality Act contains a section on Access which explains that access is not simply defined as being physical access to services for people with disabilities, but carries the wider definition of ensuring that all users are able to access services.

In order to create an equality of opportunity checklist you will need to look at how accessible the setting is, both physically and linguistically, for those for whom English is not their first language, or with low-level literacy skills. The below list indicates aspects of the equality of opportunity that need assessing in your audit:

- How easy is the setting to find? Is it well signposted?

How accessible is the setting? For parents with prams or pushchairs? For parents or children in wheelchairs?

Can parents bring other siblings who are not attending the sessions, when they are in need of support or information?

How accessible are the activities in the setting for a child with a physical disability? Can they be easily adapted?

Are staff suitably trained to support children with special or additional needs?

Is support available with form filling etc. for parents with basic literacy skills or limited English?

How is individual communication with parents or carers managed when they are unable to access the setting and the child is dropped of and collected by transport?

How do you support children to access the outdoor area who have inappropriate clothes/footwear?

Diversity checklist

The Practice Guidance for the EYFS recommends that settings reflect 'the ethnic, cultural and social diversity in society' DCSF, (2007) page 17. The Welfare Requirements, which are part of the Statutory Framework, expand on this with:

> All children, irrespective of ethnicity, culture or religion, home language, family background, learning difficulties or disabilities, gender or ability should have the opportunity to experience a challenging and enjoyable programme of learning and development.
> EYFS (2007), *Statutory Framework for the Early Years Foundation Stage*. DCSF, page 10

The diversity checklist that follows looks at some of the ways settings can meet this requirement of the Welfare Requirements. It is important that diversity is not tokenistic but threaded through all aspects of the setting. Providing multicultural resources alone is not enough. Multicultural resources can include dolls from different nationalities; play cooking utensils from around the world, for example a wok, books in different languages and providing information on different cultures and religions; dressing up clothes and materials from around the world and posters of the community.

Page 38 of the Welfare Requirements for the EYFS sets out what data must be recorded by settings for the ethnicity of the children attending. Chapter Four, The Emotional Environment, has a case study showing how a primary school celebrated the diversity of its children and staff.

It might be a good starting point to list the different members of your community and consider each statement or point for each group. This will ensure that practice is good across all groups and not just some. For example how does your setting support children from the local traveller community compared to those with a disability? The below list indicates aspects of the diversity checklist that need assessing in your audit:

Is there a welcome sign in all the languages of the children using the setting?

Is there a system to ensure that this is regularly updated?

Do posters reflect the diversity of the setting?

Are the settings resources and books multi-cultural?

Are leaflets on the setting available in the main languages of the users?

What support is available for non- English speaking parents?

Are Dads made to feel welcome in the setting?

Are a range of different religious festivals celebrated?

Are families from different ethnicities encouraged to share their cultures and religions?

Is discrimination by everyone, parents, children and staff, challenged within the setting?

Does the food served reflect the diversity of the children?

Policies and procedures checklist

The policies and procedures checklist focuses on the documentation your setting may require to promote health and safety and meet the EYFS statutory requirements.

Chapter five includes sample policies, procedures and risk assessments.

The below list indicates aspects of the diversity checklist that need assessing in your audit:

- Do health and safety risk assessments of the indoor areas and outdoor areas

- Are the risk assessments regularly updated? Are they displayed for all to see?

- Is the health and safety policy in place?

- Are fire evacuation procedures outlined in signs? Do you have a record of evacuations? Do you have a record of fire safety equipment? For example checks to fire extinguishers, emergency lighting, and fire alarm tests

- Cleaning records

- Procedures for recording hazards and faulty equipment

- Accident policy

- Accident recording procedure

- Are the setting's 'rules' displayed in picture format for children?

- No smoking policy and signage

- Sandpit policy

- Large play equipment policy

- Trampoline policy

- Water play policy

- Arrival and departure procedures

- Outings policy

- Equal opportunities policy (does it include the environment?)

- Procedure for informing Ofsted of any major changes to the premises

On completing these checklists you will now have a complete record of the area that you are looking to develop, or the whole setting. This auditing process will provide a good starting point for any future changes. They might also be useful if you are considering applying for funding from charities etc.

SWOT analysis

Compiling a SWOT analysis with staff by assessing the strengths, weakness, opportunities and threats facing your setting can be a good way for a setting to look at their learning environment. The analysis can be carried out over the whole learning environment or broken down into individual areas.

A SWOT analysis is often used as a tool to evaluate existing provision, when in the first stages of planning or developing a new project.

Strengths: list the positive aspects of the environment. For example, part of the outdoor area is covered by a canopy thereby encouraging all weather outdoor play.

Weaknesses: list the aspects of the environment that need improvement. For example, poor storage, the children are unable to choose their own activities.

Assessing risks

Opportunities: list things that might help to improve the environment that are available to the setting. For example, space available.

Threats: list things that might prevent the improvement of the environment. For example, lack of funding.

Now you have a real picture of the provision, you need to think about how you can develop your provision further. In the following three chapters you will find ideas on how you can improve your setting. Case studies on real settings will demonstrate how small changes can often have a significant impact on a setting and the learning for children.

Examples from real settings

The majority of the examples used in this book are from the following settings:

Woodlands Children's Centre

This Sure Start funded Children's Centre opened in September 2008. It was partly a refurbishment of a wing of a school (Gilbert Scott Primary School) and partly a new build. The Centre is large with two playrooms, an activity room, sensory and soft playrooms, two training rooms, a meeting room and health room as well as offices. The Centre has three outdoor gardens opening from the playrooms and these have all been fully canopied to allow all year round, any weather play. The children also have access to the large playing fields of the attached school. This is being developed and has already benefitted from the installation of a mini trim trail.

I manage the Centre and was appointed before the building work was completed, so have had the pleasure, along with the staff, of designing and developing the space.

Gilbert Scott Primary School

This one form entry school serves the local community. It was a junior and infant school that amalgamated in 2007, moving into its newly refurbished premises in November 2008. The Early Years Foundation Stage Unit, formed of a maintained nursery class for children in the academic year they turn four, and a reception class, is led by Donna Adams. Donna also works part time for the local authority supporting other EYFS practitioners.

Purley Nursery School

Purley Nursery is a maintained nursery and an integral part of Purley Children's Centre. It offers flexible provision of the 15 hours per week early education entitlement. It also provides a breakfast club and after school club, and is open 8am to 6pm. Children attend the nursery in the academic year they turn four. At the end of the year they transfer to one of the local primary schools.

Cotelands Pupil Referral Unit

Cotelands Pupil Referral Unit is based in John Ruskin College, South Croydon. The Unit is home to the teenage pregnancy support for the borough. The young mums can access their GCSE education, or further education in the College and their baby or toddler is cared for in the Cotelands Nursery. The Unit provides holistic support for the young mums including both ante- and postnatal care on site.

KEY POINTS IN AUDITING YOUR SETTING'S CURRENT PROVISION

- It is important that practitioners are aware of what their current early years provision offers before making any changes. Auditing provision is not just restricted to the indoor, outdoor and emotional environment but also how effective 'free flow' is within the setting, the diversity and equality of opportunity that it offers, and the policies and procedures that are in place.

- By auditing the early years provision practitioners will be able to look at what areas are well resourced and organised and which areas need further improvement and development.

- Auditing provision will help practitioners when completing their Ofsted Self Evaluation Form by providing evidence regarding the physical setting, quality of provision, how the environment impacts on the children's learning and development, and how the environment is managed.

- Completing a SWOT (Strengths, Weaknesses, Opportunities and Threats) Analysis will help practitioners to commence the process of change.

Chapter 2

The indoor environment

My happiest indoor memories from my childhood have to be playing 'cafes' with my sisters. Often we would spend as long preparing to play the game as actually playing it. We did have a few pieces of play food but we made most of the cafe food ourselves; cutting out shapes of paper and colouring them in. We made our own shop signs, menus, and even the money! Our rather large collection of dolls and teddy bears were the customers and we lined them all up in pairs down the hall, queuing to get into the cafe! We would give them handbags and purses with 'money' in. We had old china tea sets, a plastic shop till, and a small set of scales; I think we must have been the only cafe that weighed out portions of chips! We took it in turns to play the different roles: serving the food, cashier, and table waitress. The game would last for hours (we did have a large number of bears to feed!) and often take up the whole of the downstairs of the house.

There are many reasons why our game was so engaging:

- It was child-led. We chose to play it and established our own rules for the game.

- We had space. We were able to use the space we needed and it was flexible; we were able to move tables and chairs around to suit out game.

- We had access to creative resources: paper, colouring pencils, and scissors to make our food and signs.

- We were allowed to play for as long as we wanted, with no routine to stop us, allowing us to become very deeply engaged in our activities.

Research led by Ferre Laevers has shown that the most learning takes place when the child is deeply engaged:

Young children regularly become absorbed in what they are doing and Professor Laevers believes that an involved child is gaining a deep, motivated, intense and long-term learning experience. He bases his theories on the understanding that the most productive learning occurs when we are so involved with something that we lose ourselves in it. Cox P (2005) Effective Early Learning Project

But above all we had an enabling environment that encouraged us to be independent, to explore and experiment; it allowed us to follow our interests, offered stimulation and challenge and was fun!

This chapter looks at how different childcare provisions can tackle the multitude of issues they face in providing an enabling indoor environment: from making the most of the available space, to providing for children's basic needs, and complying with health and safety regulations. Each issue is considered from the point of view of a range of settings, including both home-based and group settings, as well as provision in multi-purpose settings where resources have to be packed away at the end of a session.

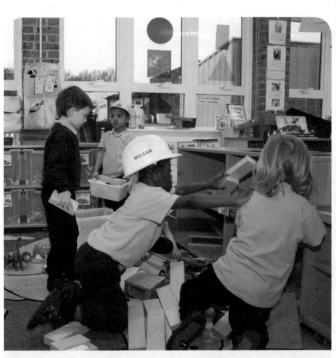

Space to play together

An environment that meets each child's basic needs

For some children, the indoor environment is like a second 'home', providing a place for activity, rest, eating and sleeping. EYFS (2007), *Principles into Practice Card: Enabling Environments 3.3*. DCSF

For children to be able to learn and develop, their basic physical needs and comforts must be met. The environment therefore needs to provide a range of minimum standards. These include daylight, or good quality lighting if this is not available (for example in a shopping centre crèche) along with ventilation and heating. Sufficient space is required for each child to play (based on the EYFS Welfare Requirements page 35) as well space to rest, relax, sleep and engage in quiet activities. It must also provide facilities for toileting and nappy changing as well as eating meals and healthy snacks, and having a drink.

Utilising space

'Indoor spaces are planned so that they can be used flexibly and an appropriate range of activities is provided.' EYFS (2007), *Principles into Practice Card: Enabling Environments 3.3*. DCSF

Planning the indoor environment can be challenging. Settings need to balance meeting the physical needs of children; providing challenge and interest; as well as ensuring that the environment is safe and secure. The EYFS framework suggests the use of 'zones' to help support the safety of the setting's users.

Undertake risk assessments and provide safe spaces where children can move freely. Create 'zones' for some activities and explain safety to children and parents. EYFS (2007), *Statutory Framework for the Early Years Foundation Stage*. DCSF, page 93

Maximising your corridors

Corridors need not be a wasted space. They can be used for displays (see page 49) but also to add interest at a child level. Providing there is more than the legal one metre clearance required in a corridor you can add toys to the walls for the children to use as they walk along. These are ideal when

children are waiting outside of a room for a session to start. These could be fabric wall hangings with pockets for the children to hide things in, interactive panels with parts to move, safety mirrors, and wall mounted lacing boards. Although these are all available to purchase from catalogues, they can be expensive. You can make your own wall activities with a small budget and limited DIY skills. Approach your local timber merchant and ask if you could have some of their off cuts. Rub them down so there are no sharp edges or splinters. Cover each bit of wood with a different material. Material can be a remnant and only cost a small amount or why not recycle old clothes and pieces of curtains etc. Wash them so they are clean and then cover the block of wood. Use a staple gun to fasten the material on the back and then secure to the wall with liquid nails. Chose different types of materials to make the experience as sensory as possible: strokeable velour, coarse hessian, shiny materials, plus materials with bold patterns and colours.

Add hooks along the wall and hang little sensory bags on them for the children to explore. You could approach your local jewellers as they often have small velvety bags for presenting their necklaces etc and might be able to give or sell some to you. Inside the bag add items that the children can explore using their senses, such as a lavender bag, a spiky ball etc.

Storage

Storage has always been a challenge in childcare settings as young children's toys are often bulky and difficult to store. There is also the added challenge of having the resources accessible so that the children can choose their own activities. Allowing children to choose what resources they want to engage with encourages them to follow their own interests and make decisions for themselves. It is important that the children have a balance between adult-led and child-initiated activities.

The EYFS, Principles into Practice Card 4.3 outlines one of the key challenges to storing early childhood resources:

Ensuring freedom for children to access resources while ensuring that they develop their understanding of tidying up and putting things back where they belong. EYFS (2007), *Principles into Practice Card: Enabling Environments 4.3*. DCSF

See-through plastic crates are ideal for storing toys so that the children can see the contents. They can also be labelled up with

The Coteland Nursery with personalised cots with their 'velcro' photos.

The day nursery at The Cotelands Pupil Referral Unit has enhanced their nappy changing area by adding pictures for the children to look at whilst their nappies are being changed. Babies are accepted into the unit from 10 days of age and staff have used their knowledge of child development and in decorating the baby room. The babies are fascinated with the images and can be seen looking at them and reaching out their arms towards them.

Cotelands also support their student mums with their breastfeeding needs. If the young mum is in college and needs to come back into the Unit to feed her baby then she is given a key fob to activate the security doors. This provides her with access without having to wait for staff to let her in or out. On the outside of the door of the baby room is a poster with clouds and a note saying 'we are sleeping'. When a baby is asleep in the nursery room the staff take their Velcro backed photo of them sleeping from the end of their cot and place it on the poster. This enables the mums to see if their babies are sleeping and they then know whether to come back later or go into the room.

Each baby and child has his or her very own cot or bed. The cots are labelled at the end with their name and a photograph of them sleeping. Above the cot on the wall is a large photo of the baby and some details. The parents are welcome to bring in a 'snuggler' or comforter for their baby and this is kept in their cot along with their own personal bedding. This enables the babies to sleep in a clean and familiar cot, which meets their basic needs and supports their emotional needs.

Cotelands Nursery have arranged their rooms to enable each room to be used flexibly around the needs of the children. All the toys and resources are movable. At lunchtime the resources are stacked up to one side to allow the children to eat at low level tables and chairs, whilst children's individual beds are taken from the cupboard and laid out for them ready for their afternoon sleep. This flexible environment enables the children's physical needs to be met in a restricted space, and also for a greater rotation of the toys and activities. It does however require a huge commitment from the staff and a continual monitoring of any health and safety issues.

a photograph of the content and the title written underneath. This will help the children to develop their literacy skills.

If toys need to be stored in a central store cupboard where the children do not have access then the children can still choose which resources they would like to play with. Make up a scrapbook or display folder containing photographs of the toys. Including photographs of the children playing with the resources will ensure interest in the book. Number the photo of the resource and the crate containing the resource. Not only will this help you to locate the correct crate in a cupboard but also help the children's numeracy development. This system works well for childminders who store their crated toys in a garage and rotate them. The children will soon learn how to use the 'toy library' book.

There are a wide range of storage units available on the market now, many of which offer deep and shallow trays that the children can access for themselves. Open shelves also make it easy for the children to see what toys are available. However, care has to be taken to position the shelves at the correct height so that children don't bang their heads on them or pull items down on top of themselves.

Providing storage at floor level makes it easily accessible to the children. This will enable them to choose their own resources easily, without having to ask for adult support.

In her home, Cherie uses her large conservatory as her main childminding area. One end is fitted out with large storage units purchased from a national chain store. The units are flexible, allowing her to fit trays of different depths, add in hanging rails (great for the dressing up clothes), and open shelving for books and puzzles. This allows the children to chose and access some activities for themselves.

Material bags make excellent bags for storing themed items. Like 'story sacks' that have a book and then various linked resources to extend the learning. The advantage with bags is that they can be hung on pegs around the setting and are easily accessible to the children. You could decorate the bag so that the children recognise which bag contains which contents, making choosing easier. For example a bag containing animal themed items could be made from an animal print fabric or with a piece of fake fur fabric attached to the front. Small pieces of fabric can be purchased cheaply from a well-known online auction site.

Using natural materials for storage, rather than plastic, makes it more sensory and interesting. Whilst purchasing storage units with

POINT FOR REFLECTION

Planning an indoor environment

When planning an indoor environment you will find it useful to follow the 'Making Changes' section in Chapter five, as it follows a series of steps to help with planning, consulting and implementing a change to the environment.

For provisions that offer separate rooms for different ages (for example a baby room, toddler room, pre-school room etc) then some of what follows would need to be adapted as it has been written for a room catering for mixed ages.

You will also need to consider how different areas of the room impact on other areas.

The easiest way of doing this is to use a piece of squared flipchart paper and draw a plan of the room. Add in permanent fixtures, for example doors, windows, radiators etc. Using pieces of coloured paper, cut out shapes (to approximately the right scale) representing the areas that you want to add, items of furniture etc.

Tack the shapes to the flipchart room, placing them how you had thought it might work. This will provide a more visual map of the room. You can make it even more visual by adding photographs to the plan.

Now look at each area and the areas that are next to it. Do they complement each other or promote conflict?

For example:

- Is the book area, where you hope to encourage children to look at books and have conversations with each other, in a quiet part of the room or next to the busy role-play area or sand play?

- Is the baby area away from the area, which is usually used for physical activities by the toddlers and older children?

Involve all the staff in planning the layout of the room. They may have seen good working layouts in other settings that they have worked in or visited, and be able to bring fresh ideas to the environment.

Clear plastic crates help children to access toys

Open storage at a suitable height

wicker trays can be expensive, it is possible to purchase wicker baskets cheaply from high street shops. If you have a parent or staff member who is good with a needle then they can be lined with different materials and made into storage/display baskets. Care should be taken when purchasing wicker items, and they should be checked regularly to ensure that they are safe.

Good storage systems that are well labelled (photographs/pictures and written labels) make it considerably easier to involve the children in the tidying up activities at the end of a session and putting things back in the right places.

The children in the nursery class at Gilbert Scott Primary School find tidying up much easier following the introduction of the 'shadows'. Shapes, slightly larger than the item, are cut out from black card and stuck to the surface. A small photo of the item is sometimes added, as well as the name of the item. They are then covered in clear sticky back plastic. The children then match the item to the shadow. This system can be used on the top of work surfaces but also on vertical boards by adding a hook at the top of the shadow.

Storage for settings in shared spaces, for example pre-schools in community or church halls or crèches in sports centres, can be more complicated, with everything having to be stored away after each session. One option with such multiuse spaces is to share some resources with other users of the premises,

for example a toddler group may use the same hall a couple of times a week. The advantages are you might have a wider range of resources to access and not have to put them all away at the end of each session. However, in practice it can create problems with resources being broken and misplaced, and so requires careful management by both parties..

Health and safety

Page 17 of the *Practice Guidance for the Early Years Foundation Stage* (DCSF, 2007) provides a list of items that should be considered when risk assessing the environment (both indoor and outdoor).

But providing a safe environment is more than ensuring the children are safe, it is about supporting the children to develop an understanding of safety and of reasonable risk taking. It is also about raising parents' awareness of risks so that they can provide a safe home environment. Below is a suggested checklist on how to inform parents about health and safety policies:

- Risk assessments can be displayed in rooms

- Display posters about health and safety issues, including road and car safety

A healthy lifestyle display

- Provide leaflets from organisations like the Child Accident Prevention Trust (CAPT) or The Royal Society for the Prevention of Accidents (RoSPA)

- Ensure the setting's policies and procedures are shared with parents, and that they are involved in the writing and reviewing of them

Below are ideas for engaging children in health and safety:

- Use visual reminders on posters around the setting about health and safety issues, for example hand washing, throwing tissues away etc.

- Involve the children in making displays for National Safety Week and plan themed activities, for example road safety

- Discuss safety with the children regularly and ensure they know how to behave indoors. (page 46 of Chapter Four discusses behavioural support).

Displays

Displays are a great way of sharing information and children's artwork. They can be used to:

- Display children's artwork

- Demonstrate to parents through photographs the different activities that the children have been engaged in

- Celebrate different cultures, religions, festivals and the diversity of the families using the Centre

- Promote messages linked to the five Every Child Matters outcomes

- Share information with parents on policies and procedures, holiday closures, etc.

Planned and unplanned changes to the environment

Sometimes there can be changes to the environment, planned or unplanned. Unexpected outdoor changes might include extreme weathers, for example a large snowfall, or emergency work when a tree falls down in strong winds. Indoor planned changes might include altering the layout of the setting or pre-booked building work. Try to make the most of any changes to the environment, especially if they are only temporary. Planning for the setting should be flexible enough for practitioners to make alterations in order to include environmental changes as well as following the children's interests. Supporting children with change is very important and discussed further in the Emotional Environment Chapter.

Supporting parents to develop enabling home environments

The EYFS places great emphasis on involving parents in their child's learning and supporting them to develop a home environment that will enhance their child's development opportunities.

'Parents can be helped to understand more about learning and teaching through workshops on important areas such as play, outdoor learning or early reading.'
EYFS (2007), *Principles into Practice Card: Enabling Environments 2.2*. DCSF

At Woodlands Children's Centre we regularly run courses and workshops that support parents to develop their understanding of how their child learns. One of the most successful has been the Croydon Adult Learning and Training Family Learning Literacy Course. The parents and children joined together for sessions to develop resources to support their child's literacy learning. The parents produced a music box with their child. Each box contained homemade resources to support the singing of nursery rhymes. For example, five yellow ducks cut out of yellow card, laminated and then each stuck on a lolly stick to help act out the rhyme. Feedback from the children and parents has been really positive and we are planning on running another course to engage more parents.

The six areas of learning indoors

The EYFS (DCSF 2007) has six areas of learning. Each must be included when planning the indoor space, just as you would for the outdoor provision.

Personal, social and emotional development

> Support the development of independence skills, particularly for children who are highly dependent upon adult support for personal care.
> EYFS (2007), *Practice Guidance for the Early Years Foundation Stage*. DCSF, page 43

How are children supported to remember the different steps they need to do when using the toilet independently? An enabling environment will include a visual prompt poster, showing the different steps. Further details of making a routine poster can be found in Chapter Four, The Emotional Environment.

Providing photos, names and even a piece of the child's own work above their peg area will help a child to identify which peg is theirs. This will help them to become more independent when they need to find their coat or bag.

Communication, language and literacy

> 'Provide time and relaxed opportunities for children to develop spoken language through sustained conversations

between children and adults, both one-to-one and in small groups between the children themselves. Allow children to initiate conversations, respect their thinking time and silences, and help them develop the interaction'.
> EYFS (2007), *Practice Guidance for the Early Years Foundation Stage*. DCSF, page 40

The teacher in the maintained nursery at Gilbert Scott Primary School, Donna, had produced a beautifully painted screen on a jungle theme. The children loved it and it linked well to the animal stories and rhymes they enjoyed. Donna decided to follow their interests and extend the screen into a 'jungle' corner for the children. She moved the furniture and added green net material to make a den area for the book and reading corner. The children participated in the decoration of the area by helping to make giant leaves and a paper snake. One child asked Donna "Where is the roof? The jungle has a roof of trees." So Donna added a net canopy over the top and more leaves made by the children. The area has become very well used, the children enjoy spending time sitting in 'the jungle' looking at books and talking. The tape machine has moved in and the children now spend time listening to stories alongside looking at books. It has been key in helping children to settle into the nursery. Children feel safe sitting in the area as it is enclosed.

Children need to see text in different formats and to understand the importance of learning to read. At Gilbert Scott

Story sacks can be hung in corridors

Primary School Nursery they have made a hanging display of some of the different places a child might see printed writing. This helps children to make literacy real and purposeful.

Problem solving, reasoning and numeracy

Exploit the mathematical potential of the indoor environment, for example, enabling children to discover things about numbers, counting and calculating through practical solutions such as finding out how many children are in the music area or how many story books a child has looked at today.
EYFS (2007), *Practice Guidance for the Early Years Foundation Stage*. DCSF, page 61,

Provide a puzzle area. Make some laminated signs to hang up with the words 'Puzzle area' and pictures of different types of puzzles, for example wooden tray ones. Provide a wide range of puzzles for the children to choose from encouraging them to progress from the simple peg shaped boards to more complex floor and table puzzles with an increasing number of pieces. For children completing the more challenging puzzles, provide space for them to leave the puzzle part completed, where it will not be interfered with by other children, so they can come back to it later.

Knowledge and understanding of the world

Use correct terms so that, for example, children will enjoy naming a chrysalis if the practitioner uses its correct name. EYFS (2007), *Practice Guidance for the Early Years Foundation Stage*. DCSF, page 76

Add an 'interest table' to your setting. Using the interests from the children, have a themed table with different real items for the children to look at, hold and explore. Provide the children with the correct terminology for items on the table to enhance their learning. The theme can be changed periodically to maintain interest from the children.

Physical development

Provide equipment and resources that are sufficiently challenging and interesting and that can be used in a variety of ways, or to support specific skills.
EYFS (2007), *Practice Guidance for the Early Years Foundation Stage*. DCSF, page 91

The Soft Play room in Woodlands Children's Centre offers a flexible learning environment. The small children can play in the ballpark, climbing in and out of it, using the soft steps and slide, learning to move in amongst the balls and to

Open boxes encourage sorting skills

The jungle themed reading corner

Experimenting with staggered building

Role playing health and safety

Ann is a registered childminder who has been registered for over 25 years and been graded as Outstanding twice by Ofsted. She recently had an extension built to the side of her house. For many childminders this would be a nightmare but Ann is turning the changes in the environment into exciting learning and development opportunities for the children in her care.

Ann cares for a number of children under eight years of age, some coming on different days. Prior to the start of the building work, Ann had spoken to the parents and the children about the plans. She risk assesses the project on a daily basis to ensure the safety and wellbeing of the children. For example she checks that the access to the front door is clear and that no tools have been left out. (Risk assessments and dealing with building works is discussed in more detail on pages 62).

The children have all shown great interest in the project. There has been a lot to see: diggers being unloaded off the back of large trucks, skips arriving and being taken away filled up, scaffolding poles being delivered and then constructed, as well as walls being knocked down and built

up again. The large deliveries of bricks and sand in giant bags being swung by a crane arm from the lorry over the building into the garden was of particular interest. Ann uses every opportunity to discuss what is happening with the children and to increase their vocabulary and knowledge. She uses the correct terminology for the processes and the tools the builders are using.

The children ask lots of questions about the workmen and their roles. Ann has explained that the bricklayers are putting up the walls and then a roofer will come to put up the roof. They are also very interested in the different equipment and tools that the builders are using. "What are they doing now Ann?" is constantly being asked by the children. Ann asks the children open-ended questions to encourage their thinking and problem solving skills, "How do you think the builder will get the bucket of mortar up to the top of the building?"

Ann and the children themselves have found very practical ways for them to use their new knowledge and understanding. The building bricks are always out now. Initially the children were building the bricks up in straight towers. Ann showed

Working together

Firm foundations

them how easy these were to knock over and break. She showed them how the bricks were being put up by the builders, staggered to make them stronger. The children are now experimenting and learning to do this for themselves. The children have started to work together in their constructions having seen how the builders are working together on the extension. They can be observed collecting the bricks in the bucket and bringing it over to the construction to share.

Ann has explained about safety to them and why the builders wear hard hats to protect their heads. The children enjoy taking turns to wear the toy hard hat whilst doing their own construction activities.

For those quiet times when the baby is sleeping, Ann has sat with the children and watched Bob the Builder programmes. The children become very animated when they recognise pieces of machinery from outside the house on the television. At the local toddler group, the ride on diggers have become very popular with Ann's minded children. She has taken the children to the library to find books to further their interest. *Dig, Dig, Digging* by Margaret

Mayo and the Usborne lift and look book: *Diggers* by Felicity Brooks soon became firm favourites.

The children had expressed an interest in the mixing of the mortar for the bricklaying. Ann organised for the children to ask the builder what the mortar was made of. They then made their own 'mortar' using sand and flour and water, copying the one to five ratios that the builders were using of cement and sand. This 'mortar' was then used to 'stick' together cardboard boxes to make a wall.

The children often link what they are doing to the building project. For example they were playing the hand game with Ann, where you take it in turns to put your hand on the top of the pile of hands. One of the children commented that they were building a tower with hands and not bricks!

Ann has really embraced the changing environment to support the children's learning and development and backed up what they are seeing with hands-on activities that are readily available already within her setting, thereby further enhancing the experience.

throw them. The giant wall puzzle provides challenge and creativity, such as what is the strangest person or animal you can create from the pieces? The selection of different shaped building blocks encourage building on a large-scale to support the development of gross motor skills.

Creative development

> Provide a stimulating environment in which creativity, originality and expressiveness are valued.
> EYFS (2007), *Practice Guidance for the Early Years Foundation Stage*. DCSF, page 105

The Woodlands Children's Centre has a small sensory room. This provides a very rich environment for the babies and children to explore light, sound, motion and aromas. Alongside the installed specialist resources of bubble tubes, fibre optic cables, and projector, we have added a basket of sensory resources. These can be cheaply purchased and add a real tactile sensory experience, similar to a treasure basket. Initially, we found that parents and staff used too many pieces of equipment in the sensory at the same time. This meant that the environment could often become a sensory overload. I organised some sensory training for the staff and we put up some signs, however it was still a bit of a 'disco' environment at times. So we produced a simple storybook for parents to use in the room with their child. We used the Centre's travelling teddy, Patacake, as the star of the story, photographing him in the sensory room using the different

pieces of equipment. The book tells the story of how Patacake sneaks into the sensory room on his own and puts everything on and it scares him. He turns it all off and uses one piece at a time. Under the photo and the text for the parent to read to their child, are notes for activities for the parent to try. For example: with the wall magic light carpet, (a rug mounted to the wall and covered in tiny lights that change colour) to lay beside it and look up. Imagine you are lying outside looking up at the stars twinkling in the night sky. Can you make a twinkling sign with your hand? The sensory room is now an engaging environment.

The staff at Cotelands Nursery had observed how much the children were learning and enjoying using the sensory room at Woodlands and decided to create a similar environment for the babies in their nursery. Although challenged by not having a budget or a separate room, the staff developed a sensory corner in the baby room. Using lights, a bubble mirror, cushions, and a basket of sensory toys they created a very special space for the children.

KEY POINTS IN THE INDOOR ENVIRONMENT

- The indoor environment must meet the physical needs of the children; light, air, space, warmth, a place to rest, relax or sleep, to eat and drink and to meet their individual personal hygiene needs.

- Practitioners need to plan their indoor space flexibly to provide a 'homely' environment and room for larger physical activities. Planning 'zones' will help to ensure the safety of the children.

- Storage needs to be carefully planned to allow children the freedom to choose and access their own resources and be able to help tidy away after use. Using photograph labels and 'shadows' makes this process much easier for young children to manage.

- Health and Safety needs to be shared with practitioners, parents and children, through risk assessments, displays and visual routines.

- Displays can be used in a variety of ways: to share children's artwork, promote diversity and messages to support the five Every Child Matters outcomes.

- Make use of changes, planned or unexpected, in the environment to further enhance the children's learning and development.

- Support parents in developing their home learning environment and in their understanding of how children learn.

Chapter 3

The outdoor environment

Some of my earliest and happiest memories are of playing outdoors with my siblings. I was one of four children and we spent huge amounts of time outdoors playing, exploring and learning. We learnt about risk taking when our elder brother encouraged us to climb trees. We experimented with 'perfume' making, using petals and leaves from the garden. We mixed earth, water and chopped grass to make 'school dinners' for our dolls, or 'mucky gooey' as we called it! We dug really deep holes, thinking we would eventually arrive in Australia, until our Dad explained how big the world was! We challenged ourselves physically with our 'puffa puffa' races and found ways to resolve our sibling quarrels without normally involving our parents. We adapted our few garden toys to suit our activities; my metal dolls pram hardly ever had a doll in it, normally earth, stones and grass.... it made a great wheelbarrow! We converted the small shed into a whole range of things, but mostly it was a 'lift', taking us and our scooters to the next level of the 'car park' in our shopping game. We explored with little supervision from our parents, discovering things for ourselves and developing independence. Our play was child-led: we were in charge of our own play and it was real and natural.

So what were the elements of my childhood garden that made it such an engaging learning environment?

● Freedom and space

● Opportunities to explore the natural world

● The opportunity to use my imagination and be creative

● The opportunity to take risks within a safe and secure environment

This chapter looks at how different childcare provisions can tackle the issues they face in providing an enabling outdoor environment and includes case studies across a range of settings.

The Early Years Foundation Stage Framework (EYFS) explains that 'being outdoors has a positive impact on children's sense of well-being and helps all aspects of children's development' Early Years Foundation Stage, Department for Education and Skills, (2007), Principles into Practice Card 3.3

Freedom and space

Plan space to encourage free movement.
EYFS (2007), *Practice Guidance in the Early Years Foundation Stage*. DCSF, page 92

Having space to walk, run, skip and hop supports children to develop their gross motor skills. However it also gives them space to let off steam and release energy. This is especially important for boys. Health experts agree that if young children are not given regular access to outdoor physical activity they may be more likely to be at risk of obesity, type two diabetes, cancer and heart diseases.

Playing outdoors gives a great sense of freedom, even when the ground area is limited; the sky above provides a great feel of space and openness. This may explain why often children outdoors are more co-operative, confident and tolerant of others. Being outdoors has a major impact on children's emotions, personality, behaviour and their ability and attitude towards learning.

When visiting Purley Nursery the children were eager to show us how much they enjoyed the freedom of being outside. They ran up and down the garden, often with their arms wide and heads up to the sky. What was so amazing was that during their several laps of the garden, round the wooden playhouse and down the slope, they stayed in their order, there was no attempt to overtake each other, the children were not racing or competing with each other. They were running because they wanted to, it was fun and they were clearly enjoying the freedom and space.

Where possible link the indoor and outdoor environments so that children can move freely between them.
EYFS (2007), Principles into Practice Card 3.3, DCSF,

Free flow is a vital part of any early years provision because it:

- Allows children to choose which environment they wish to play in

- Allows children to move freely between the environments without having to ask adult permission, giving them greater independence

- Provides a more 'home like' environment where children can normally move freely between environments

- Allows children to engage in activities for longer periods of time, without interruption, as there is less timetabled activities. The importance of this is discussed at the beginning of chapter two.

The idea of free flow sounds so simple, but in practice free flow throws up all sorts of dilemmas and issues for setting managers and staff trying to implement it, including:

- Staff deployment and ratios of practitioners to children

- The weather

- Accessibility

- Negative staffing attitudes (this is explored further in 'promoting outdoor play to parents and staff')

Staff deployment and ratios

How this staffing and the ratio of practitioners to children can be organised will very much depend on the number of children in the group, and how the setting is laid out. If the outdoor area is large and not all areas can easily be viewed then you will need to consider having higher staff ratios outdoors.

One way of ensuring that the ratios are correct at all times is to have a small whiteboard next to the door. A member of staff is positioned near this area and is responsible for keeping a record of how many children are indoors and how many are outdoors. They will then inform the room leader if there needs to be any changes in deployment of staff, for example if there is an increase in children outside.

Staff need to be flexible and be prepared to go outside immediately if called upon to. Having fleeces or coats to hand will make this easier.

For a childminder or nanny working alone it is not possible to be in two places at the same time. Therefore free flow will require

Facing a challenge outdoors

Choosing to be outside

more planning. One option is to have a small area of the garden fenced off near the door so that you can see what the child(ren) are doing and only be a few feet away, whilst remaining inside with the other children.

The weather

Ideally settings should have a covered outdoor area that allows for play outdoors all year round, and in all weathers. There are now a large number of companies offering canopies and awnings to protect the children from the elements. However they are expensive and may require planning permission from your local authority.

Limited protection can be provided by a gazebo. Most are shower-proof and some offer protection from UV rays. If it is not a permanently installed structure, care needs to be taken in windy weather.

Sun protection can also be provided naturally with shade from trees and buildings. Providing den-building materials such as large cardboard boxes and colour dyed sheets will allow the children to make their own protection. There are also a wide range of pop-up tents that provide UV protection, designed originally for use on beaches, but they make great little dens for children to sit and chat safe from the sun's rays.

Ask parents to bring their child appropriately dressed for the season. Remind them via newsletters and word of mouth to bring in welly boots, hats, mittens, and scarves in the winter, and sun hats and sun cream in the summer. For some parents they might need a regular reminder that the weather has changed and their child will be playing outdoors and needs his coat. This will especially apply to parents who drop their child off by car and have no real idea of the temperature because they have come from a central heated house into their car. Provide child-sized umbrellas for the children. Children will need to be supported in learning how to use them safely so as not to accidently hurt other children with them.

The weather provides so many opportunities for children to learn. Utilise the power of the wind by decorating your outdoor area with wind chimes, spinners and socks. They can be secured from canopies, brackets on boundary walls or fences or from stakes in the ground (subject to health and safety risk assessment). There are so many different types now available on the market, but you and the children can make your own. Wind chimes can be made from decorated ceramic plant pots, shells, keys and cutlery or kits

POINT FOR REFLECTION

Engaging parents in messy play

Some parents may not be aware that their child will be engaging in messy play. Consider how you will explain to parents the importance of messy play in their child's learning and development, through exploring textures and materials using their senses.

Does your setting's literature explain to parents that their child will find it easier to engage in messy play activities when they are wearing old clothes?

can be purchased from craft or educational supply catalogues quite cheaply. Adding wind chimes not only brings a musical interest to the environment, they can be made to look interesting. A very simple and cheap wind decoration are old CDs. The printed side can be decorated by the children with metallic paint, glitter or sequins and then a cord threaded through the central hole and hung from trees, brackets etc.

Accessibility

Providing free flow can be hampered by building layouts. In shared buildings, for example church and community halls, this can be even more difficult as you will be unable to make any alterations. Sometimes it is possible to alter the way rooms are utilised to allow better access to the outdoor provision, as shown in the following case study.

I visited a privately owned nursery. They had three rooms; two at the rear of the building that led onto a small courtyard style outdoor space. The third room was at the front of the building and was smaller. It had no access to the outdoors. Originally the front room had been used by the pre-school children and the other room by the babies. Both groups used the third room. This meant that free flow was not an option. The children were taken out at designated times, shoes and coats put on as a group, and then led through the baby room out into the garden. This had to be carefully planned to avoid the times when the babies were likely to be sleeping. For the older children it meant that their activities in the room might be suddenly interrupted in order to make the most of their time to go outside to play.

Example: dressing appropriately for the weather

Outdoor changing room at Purley Nursery School

When we were installing the Centre's mini trim trail (a selection of low level pieces of equipment, including a climbing wall, balance beams and stepping stones) on the field we spent some time considering the mud that might be walked into the Centre after the children, parents, and staff had run across the field and back. We came up with the idea of having a collection of welly boots available at the entrance to the centre for children and adults to borrow and use. We needed boots in a whole range of sizes for both the children and adults, including the larger sizes for the dads. We advertised to everyone, using posters, word of mouth and the Centre's Facebook group, that we would appreciate any outgrown wellies and then started a trail of the local charity shops purchasing as many as we could find. A year later we still get offered old wellies. Our large collection is stored in a plastic outdoor cupboard at the entrance, thereby providing easy access for everyone. As a result of our planning there has been very little mud walked into the Centre.

Purley Nursery encourage the pre-school children to find their own coat from their peg, identified with their photograph and name, but they also have a rack of waterproof coats, trousers and welly boots available under the canopy for the children to use. A mat on the floor and small chairs are provided for the children to use while changing and a member of staff is always close by to assist the less independent children. This enables the children to access all of the outdoor area, regardless of the weather.

The crèche staff at Woodlands Children's Centre were sometimes struggling to sort out which child's coat was who's when the children were going outside in the colder months. They did not need waterproof coats as the garden was canopied completely. We discussed how this could be overcome and decided that if we had a rack of small fleeces for the children to wear then they could help themselves and there would be no issues with the wrong children wearing the wrong coats. We approached the company that had embroidered our staff fleeces and they embroidered 20 small fleeces with our logo. The children loved wearing them and being the same as the staff! The fleeces all go regularly into the washing machine and tumble drier. This has made free flow much easier in the crèche for the staff and the children.

With little expense but lots of physical hard work the room layouts were easily changed around. The baby room was moved to the front of the building and the pre-school children to the rear. This enabled free flow to happen immediately, with the children benefitting through having considerably more access to the outdoor environment. The baby room was less disrupted by the children using it as a corridor. The babies were still able to have access to the outdoor space when the staff took them out.

Promoting outdoor play to staff and parents

Playing outdoors has so many benefits:

- Fresh air and sunlight, our primary source of vitamin D

- Space to engage in physical activities, using up energy and developing muscles and skills

- Reduction in stress and unwanted behaviour

- It provides an opportunity to explore, including the effects of the weather and the natural environment

- It enables activities to be done on a larger scale than indoors

- It provides opportunities for risk taking

- Greater freedom to use your imagination and to be creative

Most children are unperturbed by the weather and willing to venture outdoors to play. It is usually parents and staff who attempt to deter them because they themselves prefer to be indoors, especially if it is cold or wet. So how does a manager of a setting promote outdoor play and free flow to those unwilling adults?

Staff

The manager needs to ensure that outdoor work is included as part of their employment contract, discussed during employment interviews and as part of performance management. Rotas will need to fairly deploy staff between the environments and planning for the outdoor area covers all six areas of learning. The settings policies need to reflect the emphasis on outdoor learning and that staff have received training on its benefits.

Parents

The setting needs to ensure that it shares its policies on outdoor learning and free flow with parents, this may include posters on doors leading to the outdoor areas. Staff need to be able to discuss these policies if challenged by parents. The settings literature needs to promote outdoor play and settings might consider running workshops on its importance and benefits.

During the winter snow several parents at Woodlands Children's Centre asked if the door from the family room into the garden could be closed as it was letting in cold air and they were concerned that their baby might be getting cold. The Family Support Workers explained that the Centre's policy of free flow required the door to remain open so that the children could access both environments freely. This was especially important at this time of the year as children spend considerably more time indoors and have less access to fresh air. They politely suggested to parents that if their baby was cold to move and sit in the baby area which is well away from the door and has several large radiators. They also made baby blankets available to wrap the babies in, should they still be concerned. This was the first time the setting had been challenged on its open door policy and it was at this point that we decided we would develop a poster to be on the playroom doors explaining our policy and promoting outdoor play.

Storage

Just as indoors, children should ideally be able to choose which resources they would like to access in the outdoor environment. However, outdoor storage options can be more limited.

If storage units are on wheels then they can be easily moved inside after sessions, this will keep them secure and dry.

Open storage racks are light to manoeuvre and enable the children to easily see the contents and choose for themselves. These are great for sand and water play resources and sports equipment.

If resources are stored outdoors then you also need to consider how secure they are. Are they likely to be stolen over night or vandalised? This will very much depend on the area of your setting, how secure your garden area perimeter boundary fence or wall is, and whether your resources are easily seen from the road by people passing by.

Risk taking and safety

Help children to be aware of risks and to consider their own and others' safety.
EYFS (2007), *Practice Guidance for the Early Years Foundation Stage*. DCSF, page 96

With the high focus on Health and Safety it can be very challenging for Managers to provide risk-taking opportunities for the children in their setting. However research shows that children learn more when they are engaged in taking risks and are challenged. They are more likely to concentrate for longer periods of time and to a greater level. They will also choose to engage in these activities. It is also widely thought that if children are not given opportunities to weigh up and assess risks then they will be not be well equipped to cope with situations in later life.

So managers need to find a way that encourages risk taking in an environment that offers safety and security. Children need to understand how to behave outdoors, how to keep themselves and others safe, and about how and when to take risks.

Justify and explain why safety is an important factor in handling tools, equipment and materials and have sensible rules for everybody to follow.
EYFS (2007), *Practice Guidance for the Early Years Foundation Stage*. DCSF, page 103

Small outdoor space

For settings with a small outdoor space this presents challenges, however even the smallest garden can provide access to gardening activities.

Large plastic shopping bags (like those from IKEA) filled with soil, make great cheap planters and can be folded away when not in use. (Remember to make some drainage holes in the bottom first). Recycled car tyres, decking planks and flower buckets from supermarkets also make cheap planters.

If you grow plants that are sensory you will be adding more learning opportunities. As a child I loved stroking the velvety-soft leaves of *Stachys Byzantina* - we called it Lamb's Tongue. By adding plants that are rich in nectar you will encourage wildlife such as butterflies to visit the garden. Adding some logs and stones to a very small area can create a home for minibeasts. Rotting wood, leaf litter and a place to shelter will provide an

POINT FOR REFLECTION

Why is water play so important to children's learning?

It can provide:

- An opportunity for scientific investigation (floats/sinks, flow of water)

- A soothing sensory experience

- Connection to a natural resource

- Hand eye co-ordination and physical development, lifting and pouring

- Problem solving, reasoning and numeracy (full/empty, shallow/deep, measuring and estimating)

- A simple understanding of the water cycle and conservation

Adding water butts to the guttering encourages children to learn about sustainability. Ensure that any activities involving water are risk assessed and actions taken to prevent accidents occurring, for example lids to water butts secured so children cannot climb or fall into them.

Utilise the power of the sun to demonstrate some basic scientific theories. Take ice cubes from the freezer and ask the children what will happen to it outside under the sun's rays. You can make the activity more interesting by adding food colouring to the ice cubes.

Snow may cause settings problems with staff being unable to get to work etc, but for young children it is a great way of learning through play. Consider the learning that is happening when the children are making a snowman.

ideal environment for minibeasts to flourish. Provide the children with magnifying glasses and pots to put them in while they are being observed. Include some laminated signs, using words and pictures to encourage the children to look for different types of insects and to increase their understanding.

Example: water play

The stream - great for splashing in

Learning about water by experimenting

Purley Nursery have created a range of outdoor water play.

Using long strips of guttering propped up at different angles they have created waterways. The children can be observed pouring water into the top end, using a variety of different containers and water cans, and attempting to race the water down into the bucket at the end. They are learning how to collect, transport and pour water (which can prove challenging when using a watering can) as well as how water flows to the lowest point and around bends. They are also learning about sustainability as they have to re-use the water from the end of the cycle when the water runs out at the start.

The children were also able to engage in more traditional water play activities in the large water tray, using different pots and containers as well as waterwheels. Through these activities they are learning about the power of water, and how it's force can cause the wheel to turn. They are experimenting to see which items will sink or float, and they are learning about measurements, how much water is needed to fill different shaped containers.

They have also created a stream area where water is pumped out into a piece of guttering at the top and flows down a slight incline over pebbles, large rocks, pieces of wood and guttering. This provides the children with a great splashing environment! The children know that they need wellington boots for this activity and that they have to ask the staff if they can have the 'stream' switched on. They children rush to change their footwear before joining in the splashing with their peers. They are experiencing water as a natural element. They are also experimenting, how hard do I need to jump down with my foot to make the water splash up to different heights.

The staff have collected a supply of trousers in various sizes, by asking parents to donate outgrown ones. This enables them to change children if they become wet during this activity.

These three different water play activities provide the children at Purley with an opportunity to explore water on different scales, testing out their theories using a variety of methods and developing their physical skills.

Filling several bags with different materials, sand, soil, rocks, gravel and bark, for example, provides the children with the opportunity to explore them using their senses. Adding some containers, scoops, spoons, or shovels enables some large-scale physical activities with the children filling and emptying them with the different materials. This idea could be expanded into role play, by adding a shopping till, as the landscape part of a garden centre.

Mark making in a small garden can be incorporated by adding chalk boards mounted on legs and installed into the ground or attached to walls or fencing. A plastic crate with chalks and a cleaner can be easily carried in and out by the children when needed.

A small space can still enable children to develop large motor skills. Fasten a heavy-duty string or washing line across the space. From this line hang down cords with plastic hollow balls on the end of each. Provide the children with plastic rackets and encourage them to hit the balls. The balls need to be spaced so that the risk of the children hitting each other is reduced. The line may need to be adjusted so that the balls are unlikely to hit the children in the face and hurt them.

No outdoor space

The EYFS Welfare Requirements state that:

> In provisions where outdoor play space cannot be provided, outings should be planned and taken on a daily basis (unless circumstance make this inappropriate, for example unsafe weather conditions).
> EYFS (2007), *Statutory Framework for the Early Years Foundation Stage*. DCSF, page 35

If your setting has no outdoor space then you will need to plan carefully how you are going to provide alternative outdoor provision for the children and access to large physical activities.

Finding different outings for children within a close proximity of your setting, allowing the children to be transported on foot or in pushchairs, can be a challenge.

Most settings should be in walking distance of one of the 3600 Children's Centres across the country. Children's Centres are required to work with the local community and other childcare providers within their reach area. Many will have well equipped outdoor and indoor provision, that they may be able to timetable access to for your setting.

Local primary schools might also be able to offer access to some secure outdoor space when their own children are not using it at playtime or for sports sessions. This would also greatly support transition to school for the children, as they will become familiar with the school environment, making it easier when they start at the school. Other places to visit might include local parks, playgrounds, woods or farms (animals and pick your own).

Sustainability

Practitioners should be considering how to make their setting sustainable and how they can help young children learn about the environment and sustainability.

'Place' is a key section of the EYFS' area of learning, Knowledge and Understanding of the World, and includes guidance on the environment with suggested activities to support children to design and care for their own environment. See page 86 of the Practice Guidance document for more information.

Boundaries

It is important that boundaries are secure, to stop the children from leaving the site but also to prevent unwanted people getting in. These need to be checked at the start of every session. Boundary walls and fences can also be used to support the learning environment.

Large play equipment

Large play equipment will support children to challenge themselves, develop gross motor skills, and learn about risk taking. Settings need to ensure that their insurance policy covers them for the use of large play equipment and if they require written parental permission. Some insurance companies no longer provide cover for bouncy castles and inflatables.

Large trampolines are popular outdoor resources especially for childminders, however they need to be carefully managed to ensure the children's safety. Involve the children in establishing some rules for the apparatus and make up laminated posters to attach to the safety netting using words and pictures.

The case study on the page 35 looks at how large equipment can be safely used within an early years setting.

Example: risk taking

Donna supports the children to ensure their 'steps' are safe before they attempt the fireman's pole

The EYFS Unit at Gilbert Scott Primary School wanted to develop their outdoor space by introducing a piece of equipment that would support the development of gross motor skills, improve co-ordination and balance. The children already had access to the low-level mini trim trail in the attached children's centre. However, this was not challenging enough for the more physically able children. The playground surface was already a soft safety surface so there was the option of installing a piece of higher-level equipment.

After some discussion an adventure climber was installed, with different sides; nets, ropes, bars and a 'fireman's pole'. The installers thought that maybe the equipment would be too challenging for the children.

The Lead for the EYFS Unit, Donna Adams, talked to the children about how to keep themselves safe on the equipment. She spoke about them going as far as they felt comfortable with and about taking risks. Safety and supervision was discussed by the whole staff team: teachers, teaching assistants and dinner supervisors.

The staff observed the children using the equipment. Within two weeks a few of the more physically able children had developed their own methods and reached the top of the climber. They had shown a real determination to succeed; they wanted to reach the top. Some had taken reasonable risks to achieve it, climbing and then stretching over onto the other side of the frame, securing one hand and foot then releasing the others to move across. They had even used each other to help climb the frame.

Some of the children were observed making a pile of wooden blocks to climb up onto the frame. Donna spoke to the children about safety and then worked with them to develop a safe way of using the blocks, making a stair like structure up to the climbing frame.

Each year there is a new intake of children into the nursery class. The staff show the new children around the outdoor environment and explain to them the safety issues when using the climber. They ask the children "What makes safe climbing?" As the staff are unaware of the new children's abilities and limitations they are more closely supervised.

Outdoor mirror play encourages creativity

Numbered parking bays

Dens

Provide a variety of different materials and resources that will allow the children to make dens. These might include large cardboard boxes (check there are no sharp staples that the children might catch themselves on), pieces of material, old rugs, pegs, and rope. Flat clothes airers make great frames for dens and can be easily stored when not in use.

Dens allow children to use their creative skills, as well as playing an important part in developing independence and social skills. Dens provide a 'child only' place, where adults are only permitted to observe from a distance; place to be alone with peers, to chat and play. Agree with children what resources they can take from the setting out into their den area to make it more comfortable.

Outdoor role play

If role play is outdoors it has the scope to be on a much larger scale. Indoor role play normally has to be on a reduced scale, often using toy versions of items. Outdoors the space permits using 'real' resources. For example, in a mechanic role play area outside real tyres could be used. This allows the children to gain real experiences about the feel and weight of the tyres.

Babies outdoors

Some settings are reluctant to take babies and small toddlers outside unless they are securely strapped into a buggy. Providing planning and thought has gone into making the outdoor space suitable for this age, there is no reason why they should not spend time enjoying the space.

At Woodlands Children's Centre we had purchased a large wooden sand box. During the first winter we emptied out the sand and cleaned it, filling it with plastic balls instead. This provided the garden with an outdoor ballpark that was covered by the canopy. The crèche staff have found it ideal when working with babies. It provides a safe place for them to sit, supported by the balls, safe from the older children riding their tricycles but benefitting from being outdoors with everyone.

The six areas of learning outdoors

The EYFS (DCSF 2007) has six areas of learning. Each area must be taken into consideration when planning the outdoor space, just as you would for indoor provision. It is important to remember that each area is equally important and they can not

A book box should be part of the outdoor environment

Communication, language and literacy

Plan an environment that is rich in signs, symbols, notices, numbers, words, rhymes, books, pictures, music and songs that take into account children's different interests, understandings, home backgrounds and cultures.
EYFS, (2007), *Practice Guidance for the Early Years Foundation Stage*. DCSF, page 40

Gilbert Scott Primary School Nursery have added some second-hand tyres to a small area of grass to make an outdoor story telling area. A blanket is added, so children can choose to sit on the tyres or the floor to listen to a story.

Provide books and some seating, (rugs or chairs) outdoors so that children can access books independently.

Purley Nursery have a table and chairs under their canopy. On the table is always a selection of mark making and tools for the children to use; pens, pencils, paper, glue etc. This enables the children to have access to mark making outdoors all the time.

be delivered in isolation as they are dependent on each other. These are just a few simple ideas on how to ensure that you enable learning across all six areas in your outdoor space.

Personal, social and emotional development

Create areas in which children can sit and chat with friends, such as a snug den.
EYFS, (2007), *Practice Guidance for the Early Years Foundation Stage*. DCSF, page 31

The large wooden playhouse in the garden at Purley Nursery provides the children with a permanent place to be alone with their peers to chat and play. Whilst the staff supervise the children, it is from a distance, thereby giving the children space to be independent. This will support them to develop their social skills and understand the rules for being together with other children.

Provide beanbags that can be used outdoors. Ideally they need to be plastic coated so that they're easy to clean and waterproof. Encourage the children to move the beanbags to corners or small areas within the outdoor space to make a special place to sit, away from the more physical activities and noise.

Problem solving, reasoning and numeracy

Recognise the mathematical potential of the outdoor environment, for example, for children to discover things about shape, distance and measures through their physical activities.
EYFS (2007), *Principles into Practice Card: Problem Solving, Reasoning and Numeracy*. DCSF

Being outdoors enables you to allow for opportunities to learn about numeracy on a larger scale and that require greater physical involvement.

Print off A4 sheets with numbers 0-9 on them. Laminate to make them more durable and then use them for activities around the outdoor space. For example, you could position the numbers on blocks and ask the children to ride around on tricycles or scooters and collect them all in the right order. This will help the children to recognise the numbers, as well as count in the correct order. The activity also provides opportunity for children to learn about distance and measurements, as well as practice their physical skills in controlling the tricycle or scooter.

The outdoor environment

Example: an eco garden

Gardening involves getting soil on your hands!

Getting braver with the chickens!

At Woodlands Children's Centre we wanted to create an eco garden that embraced sustainability, recycling and learning about the environment as many of our families live in temporary accommodation in blocks of flats with no outdoor space.

We made flower beds from kits and also used some old blue Ikea bags as planters. The children began digging and preparing to plant seeds of fruits, vegetables and flowers.

We were then offered chicken eggs to hatch in an incubator. Originally we had not intended to keep them, planning to return the chicks to the farm, but realising the potential learning for the children we invested in a coop and three of the hens remained at the Centre. The children, parents and staff watched and learned as the fluffy chicks, of all different colours, developed their feathers and wings. We learned about their eating habits and how to clip their wings to unbalance their flight. The children now run freely with the chickens and are fascinated when they collect the eggs each morning with us. The animals have since increased; we now have 2 guinea pigs and 2 rabbits, all providing great learning opportunities.

The eco garden also includes making compost and recycling the rainwater from the roof and canopies. The water butts provide the water for the garden area and the children enjoy filling up their small watering cans using the tap at the base of the water butt.

We added craft activities to the project, for example making bird feeders during national bird feeding month in February. We found the Woodlands Trust website offered lots of ideas for activities for children and families.

A display board in the activity room displayed some of the children's crafts and photographs showing them at work in the garden. It helped the children to track the progress of the growing, especially the sunflowers! A display was made for the windows, showing the process that happens inside a chicken's egg during the three weeks in the incubator. A risk assessment for the chickens and signs reminding everyone to wash their hands after being out in the eco garden are displayed in the windows and by the door. We extended the eco project to include a farm shop role play area. See page 41 for the example.

Numeracy is added to the outdoor area at the Purley Nursery by making numbered parking bays for the scooters and tricycles. This enables the children to use numeracy in a purposeful way, to recognise the numbers, and hear them being used.

Physical development

> Provide equipment and resources that are sufficient, challenging and interesting and that can be used in a variety of ways, or to support specific skills.
> EYFS, (2007), *Practice Guidance for the Early Years Foundation Stage*. DCSF, page 91

Provide resources that help the children to develop balancing skills, such as stilts, blocks and benches to walk along. Provide large-scale building blocks, either wooden or plastic. The outdoor space allows for larger construction activities than an indoor space would normally allow.

The reception class at Gilbert Scott Primary School enjoy playing with tyres. The children use tyres in a variety of ways: rolling, stacking, climbing inside, and transporting them. The children learn to assess the risks they are taking when playing and transporting the tyres.

Knowledge and understanding of the world

> Make effective use of the outdoors, including the local neighbourhood.
> EYFS, (2007), *Practice Guidance for the Early Years Foundation Stage*. DCSF, page 75

Make bird feeders with the children and hang them up outside. Build a 'hide' with the children using a large cardboard box or pop-up tent with a sheet. Make binoculars to use in the hide using kitchen rolls. Watch for the birds coming to eat the food and photograph them to use later in a scrapbook and research what they are. Place logs and large stones around the perimeter of the garden. These provide 'homes' for a variety of minibeasts. Using giant magnifying glasses help the children to identify the different insects.

Creative development

> Provide a stimulating environment in which creativity, originality and expressiveness are valued.
> EYFS, (2007), *Practice Guidance for the Early Years Foundation Stage*. DCSF, page 105

The outdoors provides space to do some large creative projects individually or in groups.

Provide the children with sponge rollers, large decorating paint brushes and trays of water. Demonstrate to them how to use the tools on the fences, walls or ground. Encourage them to make patterns with the water.

Introduce music to your outdoor space. You can purchase outdoor music panels each containing a different type of instrument, for example a glockenspiel, however they can be very expensive (anything from £300 to £1,000 a panel). With a few DIY skills you can create your own music resources.

The nursery and reception staff at Gilbert Scott Primary School have made their own outdoor music area by using recycled household objects. They have used parts of a wooden clothes airer as a scraper, as well as metal-ridged piping tubes, saucepans and frying pans to make a variety of instruments. They purchased different types and lengths of metal table legs from a DIY store and attached them to a shelf on the fence. This made a type of chime bar. The children use wooden spoons to hit the legs with and make music.

Involving parents in their child's learning

> Parents and practitioners have a lot to learn from each other. This can help them to support and extend children's learning and development.
> EYFS (2007), *Principles into Practice Card: Parents as Partners 2.2*. DCSF

There is growing emphasis on supporting parents to develop a good understanding of how their child learns as research has shown that "a stimulating home learning environment at age 3-4 years is linked to long-term gains in children's development". *Effective Pre-school and Primary Education Project*, Institute of Education, University of London, (2008).

Example: giant weaving

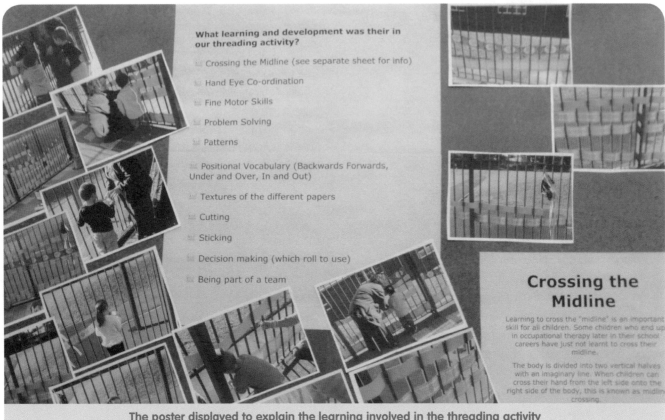

What learning and development was their in our threading activity?

- Crossing the Midline (see separate sheet for info)
- Hand Eye Co-ordination
- Fine Motor Skills
- Problem Solving
- Patterns
- Positional Vocabulary (Backwards Forwards, Under and Over, In and Out)
- Textures of the different papers
- Cutting
- Sticking
- Decision making (which roll to use)
- Being part of a team

Crossing the Midline

Learning to cross the "midline" is an important skill for all children. Some children who end up in occupational therapy later in their school careers have just not learnt to cross their midline.

The body is divided into two vertical halves with an imaginary line. When children can cross their hand from the left side onto the right side of the body, this is known as midline crossing.

The poster displayed to explain the learning involved in the threading activity

The canopied garden areas at Woodlands Children's Centre are secured with blue railing fences. We decided to use the railings as a giant weaving frame with the children to encourage outdoor play.

Using long strips of wall paper borders and corrugated packaging we worked with the children to thread them in and out of the railings. The children were supported to attach the end of the roll to one of the rails, using sticky tape, and then to thread the paper in and out of the railings, cutting it and then fastening it at the other end.

Whilst supporting the activity we observed the children weaving. Several of the children, aged two and three years, were struggling to weave the wallpaper and cardboard behind the railings. We watched more closely. The children were trying to pass the roll of border from one hand to the other behind the rail. With their arms extended to reach around the railings and reduced vision, it was proving a challenge. The slightly older children aged four and five years were not having as many problems. So we observed what they were doing more closely and found that they were passing the roll behind the railing and round until it was back in sight before taking it into the other hand. They were able to cross their midline.

We designed a poster for the room about the activity and it prompted an informal discussion with the staff in the family room and further research, via the Internet and books, into the midline. Our role as Children's Centre staff is not just to support the children's learning and development within the Centre, but to also support parents in understanding how their child learns and ways they can continue this development at home. The Family Support Workers decided that this would be a good subject to discuss informally with parents within circle time at the end of each stay and play session. They planned some simple activities that the children could do with their parents within the circle and repeat again at home, that would help them to develop this skill.

This case study demonstrates that the Centre's enabling environment is not just for the children but also for the staff and the parents/carers that access the Centre.

Example: role play outdoors

We wanted to develop our eco-garden area at Woodlands Children's Centre into a more appealing space for the young children to access. It already offered the following activities: gardening, caring for the Centre's chickens, recycling with composting and water butts, and some simple related arts and crafts. We had noted that children spent limited time in the eco garden and that everything was very structured and adult-led. We wanted to develop the area's focus so that it was more engaging for children and made a list of the needs for the space:

- More literacy and numeracy outdoors

- Role play on the eco theme

- Support for understanding of the food chain

- Something that children could relate to and that would capture their interest

- Play in which children could lead, as opposed to the adult-led activities that the eco-garden offers

We watched some short film clips on developing outside areas and role play on Teachers TV and were inspired by ideas such as a pizza delivery shop and garden centre. We decided on a Farm Shop. Not only did this link well with all current activities but also met all the areas raised in our discussion. We discussed what the farm shop would be like and how it could support the children's learning. We produced a plan of what we needed to do. We then came up with the idea of including a 'pick your own' area of the farm shop. The children would be able to pick their own apples from a tree and collect them in a basket. We printed off images of a range of different sized apples, both red and green, and added numbers to some in order to offer adult-initiated counting games and the opportunity to compare different sizes.

The outlay for the whole activity was minimal: we only bought some cheap bags, as well as green felt to line the vegetable trays. Fruit boxes and signage was supplied free of charge by a local supermarket.

As we know that children learn the most from experiencing things for real, we felt that it was important that we included some real fruit and vegetables in with the wooden and plastic toy ones. We wanted to use it as an opportunity to encourage the children to explore and maybe even taste different fruits.

The Farm Shop increased the children's interest in the eco-garden area. We observed that children stayed longer in the area, engaging in different activities in the shop. Their learning was varied; we observed an increase in social interactions and communication between the children as they chose to take on the roles of shopper and seller. The children were choosing to do mark making on the order pads, and using their early counting skills to count out the apples.

Some parents fed back to the staff that their child was now showing an interest in the fresh produce aisles in the local supermarket, and asking about the different fruits and vegetables.

Our planning sheet for the farm shop, linking to the areas of learning

Area of learning	Activity	Resources needed
PSRN	Counting money Price of produce Weights Volume Counting eggs into the boxes	Cash register Money (coins and notes) Scales Boxes (egg and large) Egg boxes and plastic eggs
CLL	Reading signs Taking orders over the telephone	Advertising signs, pricing etc Telephone Order pad and pens
KUW	Selling different fruit and vegetables	Plastic/wooden and real fruit and vegetables Posters
PSED	Taking turns in different roles, farm worker and customer	Apron for worker Handbag/shopping bag for customer

Example: working with parents to improve the environment

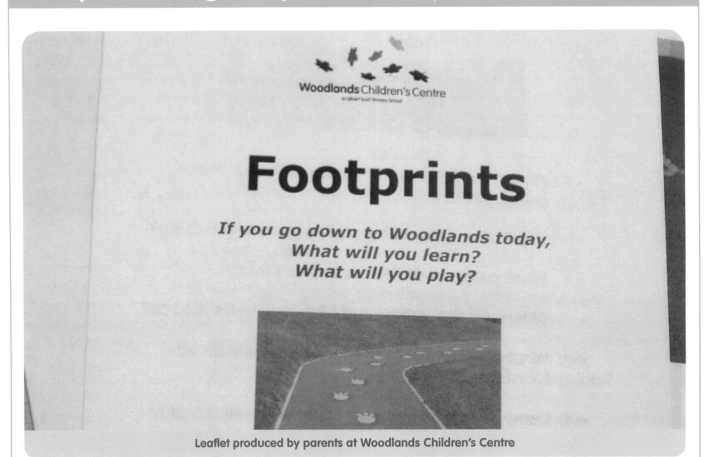

Woodlands Children's Centre
at Gilbert Scott Primary School

Footprints

*If you go down to Woodlands today,
What will you learn?
What will you play?*

Leaflet produced by parents at Woodlands Children's Centre

There is a long tarmac path leading down to Woodlands Children's Centre. Parents had asked for it to be made more exciting for the children to encourage them to come in and out of the Centre. We did some research and consulted with the parents and children and then decided to add some markings to the path. We chose yellow, bear-sized footprints and blue children's footprints. The installation process was very easy and within an hour the prints were ready to be used.

We observed the families coming down the path for the first time since the prints had been added. The children were leaping from one print to another and making up their own games.

The following week I was asked to deliver part of the Centre's Adult Literacy class as the tutor was ill. We did a brainstorming activity together, coming up with a list of ideas on how the children could play on the footprints and what learning they might get from them. The parents were quite amazed at the number and variety of ideas that came from the discussion. They then turned this information into a leaflet, to be available at the Centre, for other parents to use with their children.

The following week a Nanny arrived with two children in her care. She explained that they had been following the bear prints down the path and they had arrived at the Centre. They were now going to look for the bear in the Centre. This idea led us to 'hide' images of bears around the Centre for the children to find. We added a sign at the door asking the children to find the bears. This activity proved very popular so we decided to extend the activity by adding numbers to the bears. The older children, aged three and above, were encouraged to find all the numbers one to nine hidden around the Centre. This helped to introduce problem solving, reasoning and numeracy to the activity.

Since then the parents have become much more involved in the developing of the outdoor environment. Recently a mum asked if we could have a post box at the top of the path and letters for the children to post on their way home. This proved really helpful in encouraging the children to leave the Centre happily at the end of the sessions.

Risk assessment template for outings

Hazard	Risk	Action to reduce level of risk	Responsibility and timing	Achieved/ comments
Crossing roads	Being run or knocked over	• Children taught the principles of road safety from an early age • Children closely supervised near roads • Care taken in planning routes to avoid busier roads • Use of wrists straps if appropriate		
Falling over curbs etc	Cuts and bruises	• Ensure first aid kit is carried on all outings • Encourage children to look where they are going • Younger children be more closely supported • New walkers to go in pushchairs for outings		
Weather	Sudden change, rain, snow or extreme heat	• Ensure water is available to prevent dehydration • Sun hats to be taken in summer months and sun cream • Weather forecast to be checked prior to commencing outing and suitable attire worn		
Animal faeces	Infection and disease	• Staff to be vigilant when walking with children • Discuss with children about looking where they walk and not walking in faeces		
Lost child	Child goes missing	• Refer to the setting's lost child policy and follow procedures • Children to be closely supervised at all times • Reduced child to staff ratios • Staff to carry mobile phones		

KEY POINTS IN THE OUTDOOR ENVIRONMENT

• The outdoor environment provides children with space to explore, use their senses, develop larger physical skills, take risks and use the weather as a resource. Free flow will require planning and resourcing but provides children with greater freedom to move between environments. Providing suitable clothing for the weather and involving parents in dressing their children appropriately will help to support free flow.

• The weather can become a learning resource through rainwater puddles, wind chimes and spinners.

• Risk taking needs to be managed in the outdoor area so that children are supported to take reasonable risks in a secure and supervised environment.

• Nature and sustainability should be encouraged within the outdoor environment through planting and harvesting, caring for plants and creatures, and recycling.

• Settings with no or limited outdoor space will need to plan daily outings and opportunities for large physical activities.

• Activities can be done on a larger scale outdoors, with giant mark making and art projects, large physical activities, for example climbing frames, and real resources in role-play areas.

• Providing den-making equipment will support the children's learning in construction and also provide them with their own space to be independent and to be alone or with peers.

Chapter 4

The emotional environment

Reflecting diversity within the setting

Supporting children to understand feelings

It is vital that the environment promotes emotional wellbeing and provides stability for the children.

Children need:

- a safe and secure emotional environment in order to learn and develop. It provides them with the confidence to explore and overcome challenges.

- to know that their feelings are accepted, they will then learn to express their own feelings, maybe of sadness, anger or frustration.

- adults that will support them with how they are feeling, showing empathy.

- a warm, welcoming and accepting environment.

- an environment that embraces differences in gender, ethnicity, language, religion, culture, special educational needs, and disabilities.

- support to develop their independence skills.

Why focus on the emotional environment?

A child's social and emotional development has significant implications for their current and later social functioning, as well as educational, and employment success. If emotional development is fostered at a young age, children are more likely to settle well into school, work cooperatively, confidently and independently, and behave appropriately. A child with poor social and emotional development is at risk of poor relationships with peers, academic problems, later involvement in crime and developing physical health, and adult mental health problems.

> Key to social and emotional development is the child's early relationship with parents or caregivers. Efforts to support parents in understanding and fulfilling their children's emotional needs can help to provide a secure base from which children grow into well-rounded, capable adults with robust mental health.
> DCSF (2009), *Every Child Matters*

This chapter looks at how different childcare providers can tackle the issues they face in providing an enabling emotional environment and includes case studies across a range of settings.

Welcomes

> The emotional environment is created by all the people in the setting, but adults have to ensure that it is warm and accepting of everyone.
> EYFS (2007), *Principles into Practice Card: Enabling Environments 3.3*. DCSF.

Have you ever walked into a new environment and found it cold and unwelcoming? Maybe you have even felt ignored while the staff discussed last night's TV programmes. Did you go back again to that place? Probably not! Creating a welcoming environment is relatively easy to achieve. There are lots of different ways of welcoming children and parents to settings.

Meet and greet

This role is often overlooked and its importance not recognised. It is vital that everyone arriving at the setting is greeted with a friendly smile and a warm welcome. Using children's and parent's or carer's names makes the greeting more personal. Familiar faces can also make a big difference and be a great help in settling children. Providing welcome packs of useful information and tours of the setting when families first visit the setting are also very important.

At Woodlands Children's Centre we were aware how important families' first impressions of the Centre were and that it could make the difference between them coming back again or not. We worked together to develop a routine whereby all new families were given a personalised guided tour of the Centre

by one of the Family Support Workers. This enabled the staff to start building a relationship with the parent and child and to explain the services available that would be of most interest to them. A welcome pack was developed containing information on the Centre, a current timetable and a registration form. We produced a 'welcome questionnaire'. This allowed us to gain feedback from parents as to how effective our welcome was. When we analysed the results of the questionnaires over a six-month period it clearly showed that the parents who were given a personalised tour (approx. 95%) had felt very welcome, were better informed of the services available, and more likely to return than those that had not had a tour. Our questionnaire included some simple graded questions, for example, "How welcome were you made to feel? Very welcome, welcome or not very welcome". More open questions included asking; "How could we make the setting more welcoming?"

Welcome signs should be in different languages and reflect the diversity of the community the setting works with. You can purchase welcome signs in different languages or make your own more personal sign using the setting's logo. Why not involve your parents who speak different languages to help with the translations? You could also include a welcome in Makaton or British Sign Language.

Photographs and names

Children feel very special if they can see their photograph up on a board with their name. It gives them a sense of belonging and ownership. Some settings add the child's photo or a piece of their artwork above their peg where they hang their coat and bag.

For settings that carry out home visits before children joining, ask the child to give you a drawing they have done and have it displayed in their room or above their peg for their first day. Having something from home, familiar, already in the setting can make the transition much easier.

A large pre-school is based in a local church hall where the children having varied attendance patterns. The setting staff were struggling with how to display the children's names and photographs without any permanent display boards. As the hall was a shared space with other users and church groups the pre-school would also have faced confidentiality and safeguarding issues in displaying the children's names and photographs in a public space.

The manager purchased a portable tabletop display board that could be stored after sessions in a cupboard. The photograph of each child was taken on a digital camera and printed along with their name. Each child's name and photo were laminated together. On the rear a small piece of sticky backed Velcro was attached. (This can be purchased cheaply by the metre from curtain and fabric shops).

Before the pre-school opened each morning a member of staff would place on a table the photographs and names of the children who were due to attend that session. The display board was placed on a low-level table so that the children could reach it unaided. As each child arrived at the pre-school with their parent or carer they were encouraged to find their name and photograph and 'stick' it to the display board.

This resolved the pre-schools problems and supported the children to feel welcome in the setting. The manager then extended the idea by adding photographs of the staff to the board, ensuring they were changed each day to reflect who was working. This enabled the children to see who they would have caring for them when they arrived.

Staff and key workers

[E]nsure that each child has a key person.
EYFS (2007), *Principles into Practice Card: Personal Social and Emotional Development*. DSCF

Staff play a very big role in making the emotional environment positive for the children. They have the responsibility of meeting the physical needs of each of their children, but also of responding to their emotional needs, supporting them to understand their feelings, develop positive attitudes and promote good behaviour.

Staff will need support in their role as a key worker. Regular supervision with a worker trained in active listening and supervision skills will offer some help to practitioners who may be feeling overwhelmed by a child who is requiring intense emotional support. Without this they may become drained or burnt out and unable to offer the child the emotional environment he or she needs.

Supporting positive behaviour

Children need to be aware of the 'rules' of the setting. Understanding the boundaries and what is expected of them

helps children feel safe and secure. They are more likely to learn and develop in an environment that supports children to manage their behaviour and where they have an awareness of the consequences of their actions.

The emotional environment can further support the children to manage their behaviour. Visual reward charts provide children with goals, how they are doing and how their peers are doing. It can provide reassurance to children as well as motivation.

Donna, the EYFS Unit Lead at Gilbert Scott Primary School, wanted to introduce a new behaviour chart for the children. She had been using smiley faces but felt it was time for something that would be more interesting to the children. Following a visit to West Thornton Primary School, Donna produced a behaviour chart similar to the one they used.

This behaviour chart is based on a roadway. Each child's photo is on a car, and each car moves along the roadway depending on their behaviour. The traffic lights system clearly shows which children are behaving well and which are struggling. Children on the red light are given opportunities to change by answering questions related to their behaviour, for example "What makes good sharing?", and then demonstrating good behaviour. They can then progress from red to amber and green, and even into the 'super stars lane' for outstanding behaviour, helping and being a good friend etc.

The children have been very interested in the roadway and where their car is positioned. There has been a noticeable increase in good behaviour.

Reflecting diversity

Diversity can be reflected in many ways, for example in the welcome signs discussed earlier in this chapter, through resources; toys and books; posters and information leaflets in different languages.

It can also be reflected in community projects where everyone has been involved in the making of something. This creates a sense of belonging for those who have taken part, and being part of a community where everyone's contributions are valid and welcome.

In the reception area of Cotelands Nursery is a Community Quilt. This has been made by the young parents attending

The community quilt at Cotelands Nursery

the unit and the staff. The quilt has footprints in paint of the students' babies. The reception area is also home to another community project, a tree mosaic made by the students themselves. These two projects play an important part in the emotional environment of the Unit, bringing everyone together.

Gilbert Scott Primary School wanted to celebrate the diversity of different nationalities of the children and staff working within the school. A list was compiled and a flag bought for every different country represented. The flags hang from the ceiling in the main school reception and all down the main school corridor. This helps the children with a sense of belonging and feeling acknowledged. For some it must also be comforting to see their home flag being displayed in their school.

Making choices and following interests

In order for children to be able to make decisions in their adult life they need to start making small decisions or choices from a young age. It is important that the environment is organised so that children have the ability to choose. This will impact on how toys are stored within your setting. In the

POINT FOR REFLECTION

Coping with changes to the environment

It is good to make changes in the environment as it keeps the children and staff interested, however you do need to be aware of any issues this may cause.

Children with some disabilities do not cope well with any changes. For example a child with autism will not cope well if they arrive at the setting to discover the chair they always sit in has been moved elsewhere. If the changes are necessary then they must be carefully planned and the individual children concerned prepared for the changes to support them through the transition.

Children with visual impairments also need the setting's furniture and large resources to remain in the same layout so that they can be confident in moving around and not bumping into things.

In the next chapter, Developing the Environment, the change process is looked at in detail.

chapter on the indoor environment, there are some useful ideas on storage that enable children to self-select toys and activities.

Children also need to know that they can return to their creative work at a later stage,

> Have a 'holding bay' where 2D and 3D models and works can be retained for a period for children to enjoy, develop or refer to.
> EYFS (2007), *Practice Guidance for the Early Years Foundation Stage*. DCSF, page 110

On our visit, some of the children in the Reception class at Gilbert Scott Primary School were making junk models from plans that had drawn at the previous session. Along a shelf were the models some of the other children in the class had made during previous sessions. These were being kept so that the children could return to them, add more parts or paint and decorate them. Because the children could see their models they knew they had been kept. They may well have felt different if they had been stored in a cupboard out of sight.

Example: establishing rules in a home-based setting

House rules in pictures

We take our shoes off indoors

We play nicely with the toys, share and are polite

We eat and drink at the table

We treat the furniture with respect

An example of a childminder's 'House Rules' poster

Childminder Jane was finding it hard to get her minded child, Jack (two years) to understand the basic 'rules' of her home. Her own daughter Annie (three years) was also pushing the boundaries. Her Childminding Network Co-ordinator, during one of her routine support visits, suggested that Jane make a poster of her 'rules' using pictures. Whilst Jane had a written set of rules in her portfolio, neither of the children had seen them and both were too young to be able to read them. So Jane's Co-ordinator suggested making a pictorial rules poster for the children.

Jane made a poster on her computer using clipart images. She kept it really simple and focused on just four main areas:

- Walk in the house, no running

- Shoes to be removed at the front door

- No jumping on the sofa

- Sit at the table to eat and drink

She printed out two copies of the poster and laminated them to make them more durable. She then sat with the two children and asked them what they thought each picture might mean. Using open-ended questions she checked their understanding of the 'rules' and they agreed the consequences if they were to break them. The posters were then displayed, at the children's eye-level, in the two rooms most used by the children.

When the Childminding Network Co-ordinator revisited Jane six weeks later, the posters were clearly displayed. During the visit she observed Jack running across the room to pick up a toy and Annie calling to him "No running Jack" and tapping the poster of the rules. Jack and Annie then explained the pictures on the poster to the co-ordinator. They were demonstrating that they now understood the 'rules' of the setting. Jane's home was now a happier and safer environment for the children to learn and develop in.

Following this success, Jane is now working on visual timetables to use with the children. See page 49 for more information on visual or pictorial timetables.

Valuing the children

The EYFS principle 'A Unique Child' is important in the valuing of children, recognising them as 'competent learners from birth who can be resilient, capable, confident and self-assured.
EYFS (2007), *Practice Guidance for the Early Years Foundation Stage*. DCSF, page 5

The National Strategies' document, *Social and Emotional Aspects of Learning (SEAL): Improving behaviour, improving learning* (2005) has lots of good resources that can be used to support children's social and emotional aspects of learning, self-awareness, managing feelings, motivation, empathy and social skills. One of their resources is a birthday box. A medium-sized box is wrapped in birthday wrapping paper. When a child is given the box they look in the top, into the box and see themselves reflected in the mirror which has been fixed to the base of the box.

Personal space

Children need a place to sit alone sometimes, or a place to chat with their peers, maybe away from adults. Creating den like places indoors can be challenging when space is limited. By using material drapes and some cushions, even a small corner can take on the feeling of being a special place. It is also possible to create this in your imaginary area.

The children at Purley Nursery can really 'escape' in their imaginary space, the moon, the planets… for they have a space area, the inside of a spaceship! The children can dress up as an astronaut and use the ICT equipment (keyboard and headphones) to fly their ship wherever they want to go! The material draped over the area makes it cosy and special for the children to play in.

Some children like to bring in items from home to keep with them, but not necessarily to play with when they are there. These items, along with their art and craft work that will be taken home, needs a safe place to be kept that is easily accessible to a child. For a childminder, with just a few children, then a box with a lid would be ideal. This could be a shoebox which the child has decorated themselves. For settings with large numbers of children shoeboxes might be more difficult to store. Having a drawstring bag hanging on their coat peg might be a workable alternative.

Celebrating effort and achievement

The emotional environment needs to celebrate the effort and achievements of the children. This will have a positive impact on their self-confidence and self-esteem. This can be done in a variety of ways, for example by displaying children's artwork and ensuring that it is named (adding their photo will give it even more power). Displaying awards or certificates each week for a range of different achievements and contributions or displaying a photo list of all the children who have done well on the behaviour chart for the week are other ideas.

During our visit to Purley Nursery School, the children wanted to show Ben, the photographer, their personal records of achievements. These were very easily accessible to them in a book box. Each child was able to find their own record independently as they had their photo on the front. They held them up and wanted to have a photo taken with them. The children were showing good levels of self-confidence, created in an environment that supported their emotional needs.

Routines

Ideally children should be given time to complete tasks and activities, however in settings there has to be some element of timetable or routine to ensure that all the children's needs are met. Having timetables helps children to feel safe and secure, knowing what is going to happen throughout the day or session.

Providing visual or pictorial timetables helps the children to remember what and when things are going to happen and will increase their security. Take photographs of the children undertaking the different activities that normally take place, for example carpet or circle time, lunchtime, story time etc. Print them off A5 size and laminate them. This will make them considerably more durable so that they will last for the whole year. Attach a strip of Velcro on the back. (This can be purchased from educational and office catalogues but can be expensive. You will find that it is considerably cheaper to purchase it from a curtain or haberdashery shop by the metre.)

Attach the other side of the Velcro strip to a wall or large piece of heavy-duty card. The children can be involved in attaching the photographs in the correct order. They can remove them as each event of the timetable has passed.

Developing independence

Support the development of independence skills, particularly for children who are highly dependent upon adult support for personal care.
EYFS, (2007), *Principles into Practice Card: Personal Social and Emotional Development*. DCSF

Each child in the nursery at Gilbert Scott Primary School has their own white pot. They are stacked on a shelf where the children can easily reach them. Each has their name written on it. One stuck on and the other attached with Velcro. The children know that this is their personal pot and they can keep their own belongings in there. Often they have the children's artwork in them, ready to take home to share with parents and family. The children know they can take their 'Velcro name' to the table and use it copy their name, thereby supporting their attempts at independently writing their name.

Supporting feelings

The environment can support children to understand more about feelings and explore their own. This can be done by having posters and resources around the setting that show different emotions and encourage conversations with the children amongst their peers and the staff.

To support the children to explore feelings around friendship and to encourage them to develop social skills the staff at

Gilbert Scott Primary School Nursery use the following activity each year. At the beginning of the term the adults within the nursery model good friendship and try to highlight their own behaviour to the children. For example by saying "Thank you for opening the door for me, that is being a good friend".

After staff have done this with the children for a few weeks they ask the children what they think makes a good friend. The children make suggestions, often based on what they have seen role-modelled to them and these are recorded on a poster, which is displayed on the wall for the remainder of the year. This acts as a prompt to help the children remember and can be referred to when a child is struggling with friendship issues.

A display of photos showing children and adults faces, with different expressions on them, is always available in the nursery class at Gilbert Scott. On the table next to the display are puppets, each showing a different emotion on his or her face. These resources encourage the children to think and talk about feelings and use the puppets to act them out. It helps them to recognise other people's feelings and start to develop empathy.

The soft playroom in Woodlands Children's Centre has a set of 'emotion cushions' and 'emotion dice' that the children can use to express how they are feeling. On one side is a simple face picture, showing a smile or a frown for example and on the other is the word.

KEY POINTS IN THE EMOTIONAL ENVIRONMENT

- A positive emotional environment is vital for the wellbeing, learning and development of the children. It has significant implications for the children's future, supporting them to develop into independent and confident adults.

- A welcoming environment will help children to cope with periods of transition and demonstrate the settings commitment to diversity.

- Staff play a key role in creating a positive emotional environment, supporting children to understand their feelings, develop positive attitudes and promote good behaviour.

- Managing behaviour requires the children to understand the rules of the setting, know the boundaries and what is expected of them.

- Allowing children to make choices and decisions is an important aspect of developing independence. Storage and resources need to be organised to provide the children with the freedom to choose and follow their own interests.

- Routines are important to help children know what is going to happen and visual or pictorial timetables can help children to plan their time.

Chapter 5

Developing the environment

In this final chapter you will find practical help on developing and improving your learning environment. Any improvements will involve change, which needs to be handled very carefully to ensure that everyone involved in the change is onboard with the proposals. For most people change is uncomfortable; it is your job as a leader to manage the change process, create a culture of 'we can do better', and to share your vision for the setting. Involving staff in projects from the beginning will help them to overcome concerns and issues and feel they are important in the process. There are lots of useful books and websites that deal with the theory of managing change so rather than discussing these ideas, in this chapter the focus is on how to utilise some of these strategies in a practical way within a childcare setting.

The Family Room at Woodlands Children's Centre

Making changes

Before making any major changes to the environment in your setting, it is advisable to go through some or all of the following steps.

Step 1 Auditing provision

Chapter 1 contains checklists that will be helpful when auditing your provision. Try and involve different people in this audit, as they will bring different perspectives. You could display it on a staff room noticeboard and ask staff to contribute their views.

Top tip: Use the checklist that you are focusing on and stick it the middle of a piece of flipchart paper. This then provides you with lots of space around the document to add ideas and thoughts on each of the areas. It can later be typed up or photographed if you need a more concise document for your records.

Step 2 Completing a SWOT Analysis

Revisit the SWOT analysis that you completed in chapter one. Has anything changed since you completed it? Have you

identified any more strengths, weakness, opportunities or threats as a result of reading chapters two, three and four?

Step 3 Develop a plan

Using the completed checklists and the SWOT analysis you need to consider your plan. What do you want to achieve with this change and why do we want to do it? Who will be most affected and how do we involve them in the process? How much of the process can we do and will we need outside help? And finally, how much will it cost?

The more focused your answers, the easier it will be to develop a plan. For example, if you answer the first question with a broad statement of "we want to improve the outdoor space", then it will make it very difficult to format a plan. Narrowing down the answer to the key area, e.g. "we want to provide a den area outside" makes planning considerably easier.

The Teaching Development Agency (TDA) have designed a useful tool 'The Impact Evaluation Model' (IEM) that can be used to support planning and evidence gathering. You can access this tool via the following link: http://www.tda.gov.uk/local-authority/impact-evaluation-model.aspx

At this point it might be useful to produce a needs analysis. This will help to ensure that any proposed changes are needed and will benefit the main user, i.e. the children in the setting. One way of doing this is to record what the staff feel the children need across the five Every Child Matters Outcomes for the different age ranges. This can then be compared to the audit checklists to identify any areas that have not been covered. This activity can be repeated periodically as new children will join the setting and may have different needs.

A blank needs analysis template is included on page 60 that could be used for this purpose.

Observing the use of the current environment

Another useful too when planning an environment or changes is to observe how the children use the current environment. This will help you to identify areas that are well used and those that are not, and to discover why this maybe the case. Which activities are most popular? There are several ways that these observations can be conducted.

Method 1

Each member of staff is allocated an area and they are responsible for recording the activity in that area, how many children played in it, for approximately how long? Did they return during the allocated time period (maybe 20 minutes)? These sheets can then be collated to produce a snapshot of the use of the environment. Page 59 features a template to record the tracking of the children.

Method 2

Using digital cameras take a photograph of each area at one minute intervals. Download the photos later and analyse how many children were accessing each area and for approximately how long.

The two methods above each have their pros and cons, with impact on staff's time etc. You will need to work out a system that works best for your setting and impacts least on the care of the children. Next you need to collate the observations and analyse the data. Look for trends and patterns in the observations. Are there areas that are not being played with? Why is this? Is it because the activity in the ares is not appealing, or because the children do not see the area?

Whilst managing the three to four year old room in a pre-school we noted that the children rarely used one area of the room. We observed their play over several days and realised that this area was over looked by the children in favour of

Involving the children in taking the photos

Children engaged in their chosen activities

other activities. We wondered if it was where the space was located or if it was the resources that were unappealing to the children. So we tested out our ideas by rotating toys each morning into the unused space. We used resources that we knew the children enjoyed playing with and placed them in the unused space. At the end of the week we had our answer. The space was the problem. The favourite and popular toys were overlooked too. We now needed to work out why this space was under-used and how we could rearrange the room so that it was more noticed and accessible to the children.

Step 4 Consulting

Consulting with the key stakeholders in your setting is vital. There is little point in investing money or time into making changes or developing new projects if they are not going to be of interest to the setting's main users. Giving the parents, children and staff a voice in the decision making will give them greater ownership of the project and may result in them producing some interesting and money saving ideas that had not been considered before.

Consulting with parents is relatively easy. You can use a questionnaire; to gather views or ask individually for input, recording responses. Ask what activities their child enjoys outdoors and give some examples to choose from. You can use a 'talking wall' where you put up a sheet of flipchart with the title on it and then provide post it notes and pens for parents to add comments and post them on the wall.

The woodlands choosing tree'

Consulting with staff can be done in a variety of ways: a group discussion at a staff meeting, a brainstorming activity, a questionnaire or a suggestion box.

Seeking the views of very young children requires a little more thought and planning, however their views are very important. Ofsted's article on Leading to Excellence explains that in the best settings "the children participate eagerly and with great enjoyment. They enthusiastically discover new ways to communicate their thoughts and ideas by writing messages, using pictures and telling stories." Ofsted (2008), 'Early Years Leading to Excellence'

Woodlands Children's Centre's parents had requested more large outdoor play equipment for their children, following the successful installation of the mini trim trail. We decided to consult with the children and the parents. We did this in a variety of ways so that we could gain input from the widest possible range of children and parents.

The parents studying in the Literacy class were the first group to be consulted. I spent time in their class sharing outdoor resource catalogues and discussing ideas. They then helped to develop a consultation questionnaire that we could use in the Centre. The parents wanted the questionnaire to include pictures of the different types of equipment that we were considering so that the children could share their input as well. We then made a poster of some of the items we were considering and asked the children to indicate which they preferred. We positioned it at a level on the wall so that it was easy for the children to see, and provided a pen for them to add their 'tick' votes.

We also used our 'choosing tree'. The children were familiar to this as a way of consulting with them as we have used it several times before. We labelled the different pockets on the tree with the pieces of equipment and the children were asked to place wooden bricks in the pockets of the equipment they liked the best.

We then asked for parental input using our Facebook group's discussion board. Whilst this did not yield any comments online, it helped to raise the interest in what we were doing and resulted in a greater participation in the Centre's consultation activities, as more parents completed questionnaires in the Centre.

We collated all the information from the three different consultations and used this to inform our decision.

Further ideas on consulting with children can be found in Alison Clark and Peter Moss' books *Listening to Young Children*, *The*

Mosaic Approach and *Spaces to Play, More Listening to Young Children using the Mosaic Approach.*

Step 5 Finalise plan using the data collected from the consultation

Analyse the data provided by the consultation from staff, parents and children. Using the results of this finalise the development plan. On page 60 there is a template of a simple development plan that can be photocopied and used. At this point you will need to confirm with staff who will be involved in the project and who will be taking responsibility for it. For small projects it is good to delegate to more junior staff as this will give them experience of leading on tasks and developing new skills. They may require tight parameters, clear instructions and regular checks to ensure the project stays on track but this level of input from the senior leadership team will reduce over time as they become more competent and experienced.

Step 6 Source funding

Depending on the size of the project planned it may be necessary to source funding from outside the setting. There are lots of different pots of funding available, depending on the status of your setting. Settings funded by the Local Authority may find it harder to bid for funds, however there are ways around this, for example by getting the parents to establish a 'Friends of the Setting' group and applying for charitable status. Many funders will only give money to recognised charities as they know they are required to submit annual reports and accounts (depending on income).

A good place to start searching for funding will be the voluntary organisation of your Local Authority. Many of these local organisations provide a monthly email to members which includes news on funding pots currently available and links to their relevant websites. They may also have staff who are able to support you in writing a bid.

When submitting a bid you will have a greater chance of success if you follow the suggested process, especially if you can demonstrate the consultation work you have carried out.

The Big Lottery Fund, Awards for All and Lottery Funding regularly have grants available. Visit their websites for further information, criteria, and funding application forms.

Sometimes local businesses are interested in supporting community groups and will offer funding in return for advertising. An alternative to applying for funds is to organise some fundraising events.

Step 7 Obtain quotes

If the plan involves making large purchases or building work then it is always advisable to obtain at least three quotes from different companies. If possible ask the companies if they have done any work locally that you can visit. This will enable you to see the quality of their workmanship and products first hand. It will also provide you with the opportunity to ask the manager of that setting how disruptive the installation was and any issues that arose. This will help you to plan for the work more effectively. Ask the companies for alternatives to your original plan. They may be able to offer an alternative product that will meet your requirements, but be considerably cheaper.

Step 8 Commission work

Once you have agreed on how the work is to be done and which company or contractors you are going to use you will need to ensure that everyone is happy with the final proposal before you proceed. This is especially important if you have had to deviate from the original idea due to costs etc. If you fail to do this, people may be disappointed with the final result and think that the consultation activity was purely a 'tick box' exercise. This will prevent parents, children or practitioners from participating in future activities.

Depending on how your setting is managed or governed, it may be necessary for you to seek permission from the Managing Committee, Board of Governors or a senior manager in the head office before finally going ahead with the project. Again, your consultation work will be of great help when persuading senior managers of the benefits of your proposed project.

The next step is to commission the work with the company. Ensure the price they quoted is still valid, and that it is based on your site and includes installation costs. Ideally the company should have done a site visit or survey so they will be fully informed regarding the type of soil or ground they will be installing into if it is outdoor equipment. This will reduce the likelihood of any surprises on the day, and sudden increase in costs.

Plan with the company when and how the installation or work will be carried out. It is important to remember that you are the customer paying for their work, so be assertive and ask for the work to be done when it is most convenient to you; not when it fits nicely into their work schedule. This may mean the project being delayed by a week or two, but it will be less disruptive to your setting.

Ask how long the work will take. One day? Two days? A week? And then in your planning allow for extra time. The company

An area of the garden ready for redevelopment

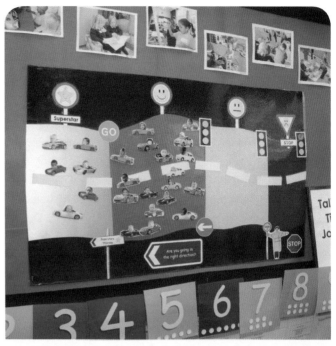

An idea adapted from visiting another setting

may be delayed on a previous job, bad weather, or unexpected problems may arise that will need to be accounted for.

Step 9 Risk assessments and health and safety

Ideally any major changes to the setting should be carried out when the setting is closed and the children are not present. However, sometimes this is not possible and therefore plans have to be put in place to ensure the safety and welfare of the children, parents and staff.

Ask the contractors to have a copy of their risk assessment of the work and use this alongside your own risk assessment. Not only will you need to consider the physical risks posed by the work, but also the safeguarding implications. Schools are normally required to only use contractors that have Criminal Record Bureau checked their staff.

For settings registered with Ofsted, it is a requirement that Ofsted are informed of any major work or changes to the premises. These requirements are set out in the EYFS Welfare Requirements under the section on premises on page 34.

Inform parents of the work that is going to be carried out and any disruption that might be encountered. This then gives parents the option to not attend if they so wish. It is advisable to include a clause in any agreement with contractors that

they are responsible for thoroughly cleaning the area after completion of work, however checks will still need to be made before the area can be used again by children.

See page 62 for a sample risk assessment for building work. This does not include everything but provides a starting point for you to consider some of the hazards and risks in order for you to develop your own assessment appropriate to your setting.

Step 10 Evaluate the impact of changes by consulting with key stakeholders

Once the changes have been implemented and the children, parents and staff have had the opportunity to experience the new environment for a while, then you need to evaluate the impact any change may have had. This can be done by revisiting some of the original consultation activities with the children, parents and families, and by asking for their thoughts. It can also be done by observing the children using the new environment and recording it, using diary notes, photos or videoing.

If you completed an Impact Evaluation Model then it would be good to revisit it now and assess whether the outcomes or impact of the project were as you had planned, or have turned out differently. It is important to evaluate both the impact of any project, as well as the impact of the entire process, at the end of any project. However, it is often a step that is forgotten. This evaluation will feed into future consultations and project plans and will ensure that lessons are learned from the project, and mistakes not repeated in any future developments.

Skills audit

It is not always necessary to pay out for professionals' services or time when making changes in your environment. Within your parents and their extended families you may have the skills or talents needed and these may be available to you for free or at a greatly reduced cost.

One way of establishing the skills of your families is to complete an annual skills audit. Consider what skills might be of interest to the setting and ask if any parents have them. For example, you might want someone who does carpentry and can make a storage cupboard for the setting. Other useful skills include web design, gardening, sewing, and fundraising. In order to get the biggest response it would be advisable to ask parents to complete it at an event at the setting. Add an incentive and you will improve the response greatly, for example by offering a free ticket to a special raffle for every completed form returned! Once the forms have been collected the information needs to be collated into a grid that will allow a member of staff to scan down and find the skills they are looking for, for a particular project.

It is not just your parents that may have hidden skills and talents. It is worth asking staff to complete the sheet too. They may have never had the opportunity to share their array of skills.

Researching other settings

When considering making substantial changes in your environment it is advisable to do some research. This can be done in two ways: researching via the internet and looking at similar setting's websites and online brochures from early years and play companies or by actually arranging visits to local settings and asking staff how they overcome issues within their environment. Often there are local networks of providers established that meet regularly at each other's settings. This networking will support all the practice within the setting but it will also give you access to a large number of other settings in the area when you can observe best practice and adapt it to suit your own setting.

Sample policies and procedures

The Welfare Requirements of the EYFS, (2007) page 20 states that:

Group providers will be expected to have written copies of any policies and procedures which are required, for example, to safeguard children or promote equality of opportunity.

Numeracy on a larger scale

Creating an outdoor music environment

The auditing your setting's current provision chapter provides a list of some of the policies and procedures that link to the environment, mainly about ensuring that children and adults are safe in your space.

Please note that policies and procedures need to reflect the individual setting, so the following documents are just starting points to be used as a base. They will need editing and adapting to meet the needs and issues in your particular setting.

Free flow policy

The below five paragraphs indicate how a policy on free flow could be written to inform parents.

We have a free flow policy in place at this setting. This means the children are free to move between the outside and inside areas for the vast majority of the day and that the doors are secured open. The children are supervised by staff in both environments.

The children are only asked to come inside for meals, circle and registration time, when the door is kept shut.

This means that we do not have a rigid timetable and short-time slots or playtimes outside. Children are able to access the outside areas all year round, regardless of the weather. We ask parents to provide appropriate clothing for their child and we have some wet weather clothing available to support this.

The children benefit greatly from being able to choose where they play. They may spend extended periods of time playing outdoors, where they may become more deeply involved in their chosen activity. This will provide them with a richer and more satisfying learning environment. All six areas of learning (in the Early Years Foundation Stage, Department for Children Schools and Families, 2007) are covered in both environments, however the outdoor environment enables the children's learning to take place on a considerably larger scale than indoors.

If you have any concerns regarding this policy then please do not hesitate to ask a member of staff.

The learning environment policy

The environment plays a key role in supporting and extending children's development and learning. EYFS (2007), *Principles into Practice Card: Enabling Environments*. DCSF

The principles into practice card defines a positive learning environment as "a rich and varied environment supports children's learning and development. It gives them the confidence to explore and learn in a secure and safe, yet challenging, indoor and outdoor spaces." (EYFS (2007), *Principles into Practice Card: Enabling Environments*. DCSF)

We continually work to develop the best learning environment we can for the children who attend our setting. This includes:

- Space for the children to move freely both indoors and outdoors and between the spaces

- Quiet space for the children to relax, chat, and read books

- High quality resources and equipment that reflect the diversity of the community

- Emotional support to enable children to feel confident

We aim for the environment to be:

- Safe: a place where children can play free from danger, supervised by skilled staff, and where they can learn about dangers and reasonable risk taking

- Healthy: a place where children can develop good hygiene practices and play in a clean space

- Supportive of children enjoying and achieving: a place where children can be challenged and stimulated, able to explore and experiment

- Accessible to all children: ensuring each child is able to make a positive contribution, and a place where every child's voice is listened to and is consulted about any changes

- A place of learning: where children have a positive disposition towards developing new skills which will support them in later life

We continually review our learning environment to ensure it meets the needs of the children. We ask parents to take part in our reviews and to participate in consultations when we are considering making changes or improvements.

We also regularly consult the children, using activities to enable the younger children to also have a voice.

If you have any concerns or questions regarding this policy please do not hesitate to ask a member of staff.

When next reviewing all policies pay particular attention to the environment and ensuring that it is included in them.

Risk assessments

Risks assessments provide a useful tool to highlight hazards and potential risks, show what actions have been or will be implemented to reduce or eliminate them, by when and who is responsible. However all too often they are written by a manager and then stored in a folder. Staff are often not fully aware of their contents, and parents and other professionals visiting the setting may have no knowledge of them.

Good practice is to have the most recent risk assessments on display for all to see. This will raise everyone's awareness of safety issues.

At Woodlands Children's Centre we have produced individual risk assessments for all the public rooms and these have been laminated and displayed in the room by the door. Please note that the risk assessments on page 61 are templates, partly populated with some basic health and safety issues often found in childcare environments. These will need to be adapted to suit your setting and additional hazards added.

For example risk assessment templates for the indoor and outdoor learning environment, as well risk assessing building work see pages 61-62. Each template includes examples of risks and hazards to consider. Other key aspects that need risk assessment in the outdoor environment include poisonous plants, gardening tools and water butts, and toys on the floor (which could be a tripping hazard). In the indoor environment you will also need to assess the availability of small toys, which could pose a choking hazard to young children.

An environment to enjoy

Learning the rules of playing together

Evaluating a project

Title of the project	
Start date/end date	
Audit of current provision	
SWOT analysis	
Consultation with: children, parents, staff and others	
Planning (quotes etc.)	
Risk assessment and installation	
Final result (does it meet specification etc.)	
Impact: consult with children, parents, staff Observations	
How could the project have been improved upon?	
What worked well?	

Tracking sheet: how is the current environment used by all children during a session?

Location and activities within location				
Date and time				
Name of staff member				
Time period	Number of children	Children (use initials)	Activities engaged in	Level of engagement
9.00am to 9.05am	6	AD, CH, MJ, BJ, LP, DH	Play kitchen	AD and CH are deeply engaged, making 'pizza'. BJ and LP are on the edge watching and talking.

Developing the environment

Needs analysis

Age group	Individual children with Special Educational Needs or disabilities	ECM Stay Safe	ECM Be Healthy	ECM Enjoy and achieve	ECM Making a positive contribution	ECM Learn and develop life skills to achieve economic wellbeing
Birth to 11 months						
8-20 months						
16-26 months						
22-36 months						
30-50 months						
40-60+ months						

Development plan

Area for development	Planned actions	Responsible staff member	Planned completion date	Funding requirements	Additional comments
To incorporate a musical element to the outdoor space (creativity, sensory)	To make a variety of wind chimes to hang outside	Pre-school Room Leader	Add date	Approx. £10 for some craft resources	Make with children as part of music themed week.\n\nUsing: cutlery, ceramic flower pots, beads, shells, keys.

Risk assessment indoor learning environment

Hazard	Risk	To whom	Action to reduce level of risk	Responsibility and timing	Achieved/comments
Hot radiators and pipes	Burns	Babies and young children	• Cover pipes and radiators • Lower the temperature of the radiators		
Doors	Squashed fingers	Babies and young children	• Fit finger guards to doors • Fit door sponges to tops of doors to prevent them slamming closed		
Wet flooring	Slips and falls	All users	• Ensure all spills are mopped up immediately • Use yellow floor signs • Wet play to be carried on non-slip flooring		
Germs	Spread of Infection	All users	• All toys cleaned on a regular basis • All surfaces cleaned daily • Soft furnishings regularly put through washing machine • Parents and children encouraged to use antibacterial hand gel on arrival		

Risk assessment outdoor learning environment

Hazard	Risk	To whom	Action to reduce level of risk	Responsibility and timing	Achieved/comments
Garden gate	Children leaving the grounds Unwanted people gaining access to the grounds	Children	• Ensure gates are secured at all times and checked each time outdoor area is used		
Animal faeces	Spread of infection	All users	• Ensure outdoor area is checked for animal faeces before use and cleared away immediately		
Large play equipment	Falls and Injuries	Children	• Children to be supervised at all times • Children encouraged to take reasonable risks but to learn about personal safety and be aware of their own physical limits • Ensure equipment is checked regularly and kept in good repair • Ensure correct safety surface is used according to the height of the equipment		

Developing the environment

Risk assessment for building work

Hazard	Risk	To whom	Action to reduce level of risk	Responsibility and timing	Achieved/ comments
Workmen on site	Safeguarding	Children	● Ask company to only use CRB cleared staff ● Ensure workmen are not permitted access to children unsupervised ● Move children to different area so not in contact		
Tools (power and manual)	Injuries	Children, parents and staff	● Area being worked on to be sealed off from children ● Workmen told to keep their tools safe and put away when not in use		
Trade vehicles on site (loading and unloading)	Knocking over people	All users	● Vehicles not to be moved on site during drop off/collection times ● Vehicles to be moved with workmen over seeing move		
Electrical cables	Tripping Electric	All users	● Only to be used when necessary ● Cables to be covered with safety mats ● Sockets recovered with safety covers when not in use		
Dust	Choking and breathing difficulties	All users, especially those with asthma	● Keeping windows and doors closed where possible ● High level of cleaning		
Waste materials	Injury	All users	● Builders told to remove waste from site as soon as possible ● Waste to be stored safely on site		
Noise	Upsetting children	All, but especially children with special needs	● Keeping windows and doors closed where possible		

KEY POINTS IN DEVELOPING THE ENVIRONMENT

● Changes to the environment have to be carefully managed and introduced.

● Consulting with children requires listening to and observing them, assessing their needs and using activities to discover their preferences.

● When organising building work, risk assessments must be carried out and consideration given to the impact on the children's routines.

● Changes should be evaluated after implementation to see what, if any impact they have made.

● Completing a skills audit on staff and parents may help to identify talents or skills that may be available to the setting free of charge.

● Researching the environments of other similar settings will provide practitioners with additional ideas for improvements and changes.

Books and websites

Clark A, Moss P, (2010), *Listening to Young Children, The Mosaic Approach*. National Children's Bureau, London

Clark A, Moss P, (2009) *Spaces to Play, More listening to young children using the Mosaic Approach*. National Children's Bureau, London

Cox P, (2005) *Effective Early Learning Project*. Teaching Expertise. http://www.teachingexpertise.com/articles/project-improves-practice-1121

Department for Children Schools and Families, (2007) *Early Years Foundation Stage: Setting the Standards for learning, development and care for children from birth to five* http://nationalstraiegies.standards.dcsf.gov.uk/earlyyears

National Strategies (2009) "Enabling Environments: Literate role-play provision for boys: audit (completed)". *Gateway to writing*. http://downloads.nationalstrategies.co.uk.s3.amazonaws.com/pdf/3895e9963638b68628161d9894e71c90.pdf

Department for Children Schools and Families, (2008) *Excellence and Enjoyment: Social and emotional aspects of learning, New beginnings*. Revised Early Years Foundation Stage version. http://nationalstrategies.standards.dcsf.gov.uk/files/downloads/pdf/9c3e1d8b4083cc43ad7acfe46196cc34.pdf

Gleave J, (2008) *Risk and Play: A literature review*. National Children's Bureau. http://www.playday.org.uk/PDF/Risk-and-play-a-literature-review.pdf

Lindon J, (2011) *Planning for Effective Early Learning: Professional skills in developing a child-centred approach to planning* (The Early Childhood Essentials series). Practical Pre-School Books

The Effective Provision of Pre-School Education (EPPE) Project: Final Report, A Longitudinal Study. (2004) The Institute of Education

Ofsted, (2008). *Leading to Excellence*. Ofsted
This Ofsted review focuses on how childcare provisions are organised, led and managed to promote positive outcomes for children and ensure they progress well. http://www.ofsted.gov.uk/Ofsted-home/Leading-to-excellence

Ealing Early Years Childcare and Play. *Literacy Learning Environment Checklist*. Ealing Council. http://www.childrenscentres.org.uk/media/File/ey/Environment%20Audit.pdf

Teachers TV have a set of short video clips showing how different settings have developed their learning environments.

- http://www.teachers.tv/videos/enabling-environments

- http://www.teachers.tv/videos/early-years-in-action-the-learning-environment

- http://www.teachers.tv/videos/early-years-role-play-setting-up-and-planning

Ward S, (2010) *The Early Years Gardening Handbook*. Practical Pre-School Books, London

Woodlands Trust's website have a large number of downloads for gardening activities. http://www.woodlandtrust.org.uk/en/learning-kids/Pages/children.aspx

Acknowledgements

I would like to thank all the settings that were used as examples of good practice in my case studies and allowed us to photograph their enabling environments:

Frances Wimpress, Head of Purley Nursery and Children's Centre.

Jan and Eleanor at Cotelands Pupil Referral Unit.

Donna Adams, Lead of EYFS Unit at Gilbert Scott Primary School.

Outstanding childminders Ann Glover and Cherie Purkiss.

I have learned a lot from visiting their settings; they have inspired me to make more changes to my own Centre and further develop our outdoor areas. A big thank you to the children, especially those at Purley Nursery School; their interest in Ben's camera, wanting to help take the photos and suggesting possible scenes, some which proved just a little too challenging: "Take a picture of us up in the sky playing with the birds". Thanks to the photographer Ben, who was so good with the children.

A very special thanks to all the staff at Woodlands Children's Centre who have been a great support and encouragement, particularly Family Support Workers Sue Walters and Sheila Clark and Outreach Worker Lisa Clements.

Finally a big thank you to my family: my husband Paul and two daughters, Becky and Amy. Without their support; cooking tea and helping with the housework I would never have been able to write this book.